A Psalm a Day

By the same author

Reminiscences of a Private Secretary
Confessions of a Business Traveller
The Gulf Region – a new hub of Global Financial Power (ed)
Reflections on Global Finance
The Wisdom of Markets and the Madness of Crowds

A Psalm a Day

A daily meditation on the Book of Psalms
through the Plague Summer of 2020

John Nugée

Published in 2021 by Laburnum Publishing

Publishing services provided by Self Publishing House

Paperback ISBN 978-1-9163873-6-2
Hardback ISBN 978-1-9163873-7-9

Contents

Foreword

As a friend and fellow member of Emmanuel Church Wimbledon and our local bible study group, I have always enjoyed John's understanding and interpretation of the Scriptures. So when he embarked on his personal journey through the Book of Psalms at the start of the COVID-19 global pandemic, and told me of his intention to turn his daily thoughts into a small book, my thoughts immediately turned to famous diarists: Samuel Pepys, with his eyewitness account of the 1660s as they happened (especially the Great Plague in 1665), and Daniel Defoe's *A Journal of the Plague Year*, recalling his time as a five year old, blurring fact and fiction.

Such a personal account, through the writing of a diary, would have been interesting in itself. But in threading his current experience of reality alongside his perspectives on God's Word in the Psalms, where God shows the weaver's loom of life, John has produced a thoroughly reflective commentary, going way beyond a personal diary.

The Psalms present us with a miscellany of images, thoughts, rhythms, songs, prophecies, sayings, emotions and perspectives on life. There is something for everybody, everyone and anyone, the collective and the individual. They give glimpses of the world that God created and works in. We are learning about God and his ways as we read his Word. We are learners as we dwell in his Word; if you like, we place an L for learner within the word WORD to show we learn about his WORLD.

John takes us beyond analysis of the structure and the form of the Psalms, to the world of enduring qualities, eternal truths, self-reflection and, above all, to be face to face with the living word, the Lord Jesus, foretold by David, Solomon, Asaph and others many years before he came to earth to die and rise again to live for ever.

This "reflection" was written by John for his own house group members to enjoy and immerse themselves in day by day during the 2020 lockdown. I hope and pray many others will find it as challenging, helpful and encouraging as I have.

Robin Linnecar

Author's Note

This book grew out of a daily email that I began sharing with fellow members of my bible study group at Emmanuel Church Wimbledon, as the coronavirus crisis came closer to Britain in spring 2020 and looked ever more likely to affect our lives radically. I decided to work through the Book of Psalms, concentrating on one psalm a day – I hadn't made any decision when I started what I would do with Psalm 119! – and to share a short, bite sized "thought for the day" on each psalm with the other members of the house group for mutual encouragement and as a way of staying in touch with each other while we could not meet physically.

The daily commentary is almost entirely verbatim from each day's email, and thus faithfully reflects my changing thoughts and moods as I read the psalms during the corona crisis – I have not tried to edit them either into a coherent statement of faith, or to avoid repetitions or internal contradictions, of which I am sure there are many. They are what I thought and wrote at the time.

My fellow study group members were very generous in their reception of my daily email, and gave me many useful comments and reactions. These are not included in the daily entries, but undoubtedly affected my own thinking as my study of the psalms progressed, and they may well detect entries for subsequent days where I have picked up on their thoughts. I am grateful to all of them for joining me in our journey through the psalms. I am particularly grateful to Robin Linnecar, whose advice and guidance throughout the summer, in the direction of the daily emails and in giving shape and structure to the book, were inspirational.

I decided very early on to add some observations from our daily life to each day's entry as the crisis hit us; they are a mixture of commentary on the life of the nation and notes and thoughts on our life at home. Like the daily reflections on the psalms, they have not been edited or massaged into a neat, consistent account but are simply my daily record of what seemed worthy of note during the extraordinary times we were living through.

Although the Plague Summer of 2020 did give way to a less constrained autumn, more recently both the virus and the restrictions on our daily lives have returned. So some of the optimism in the daily journal notes, especially the later entries, was alas misplaced. But I hope they will be of interest even so. And whether the pandemic changes, recedes or intensifies, the psalms themselves are timeless and always relevant, and I hope this book will be of value whenever anyone wants a *vade mecum* as they read the longest (by number of chapters) and for many one of the most beautiful and deeply spiritual of all the books in the Bible.

New Malden, March 2021

The Book of Psalms: An introduction

The Book of Psalms is central to the Old Testament and a remarkable body of 150 prayers and songs written over perhaps as much as 1,000 years and by many different human authors. The earliest psalm is probably Psalm 90, which is attributed to Moses, and there are psalms that would appear to be finalised in their current form during or even after the Exile in Babylon (for example Psalm 137, which is directly placed in Babylon, or Psalm 126, which starts "When the Lord brought back the captives to Zion").

The English word "Psalm" comes from the Greek Septuagint title of the book, and implies both that the psalms were sung and that they were accompanied by musical instruments. Although all the psalms can be used for private prayer and meditation, many of them are clearly designed for public use and communal praise – the Hebrew word for the Psalms is *Tehillim*, meaning praises – and perhaps the best way to consider them is as playing the same role for the Israelites that hymn books do in modern church worship.

The ordering of the psalms is traditional, and was settled quite early on. The division of the 150 psalms into five "books" is also traditional, though it is not clear what the division means and there is no agreed explanation for it – it may just be that the physical constraint of the size of scrolls meant that the Book of Psalms required five scrolls. There is a Jewish tradition that identifies the five books in the Book of Psalms with the five books of the Torah or Pentateuch, but it is not clear what the basis for this is and although some commentators have discerned some linkages with the Mosaic books, they are far from strong.

The psalms are unusual in that over two-thirds of them have an introductory note. These give details such as the occasion for the psalm, its authorship and even in some cases the tune that should be used to accompany it. They are present in even the ancient texts and there are grounds to believe that they contain authentic and reliable information, though it is not always easy to link a stated authorship with the events being described, and some of the attributions might perhaps be seen more as "in the style of" or "from the school of".

Probably the psalms where the authorship is least in doubt are those attributed to King David; he is identified as the author of 73 psalms – nearly half the book – and many of them can be directly linked to events in his life. The Davidic psalms also have a very distinctive and well-defined style, direct and impassioned. Some seven or eight other authors are also mentioned by name, the next most prolific being Asaph who has 12 psalms connected with him. Just over a third of the psalms are anonymous.

The psalms show how the earthly life of the people of Israel intersected with their spiritual life to a remarkable degree. Many of the psalms are grounded in reality, in events in the here and now, but the psalmists always reflect on God and their relationship to Him, His relevance to their daily lives. There are psalms for almost every event in the life of the faithful: Lament psalms call on God for help in difficulties, Thanksgiving psalms give public thanks for His deliverance (either already received or anticipated), Praise psalms call the people to worship, and Penitentiary psalms call out to God in repentance of the psalmist's sins and to seek His forgiveness.

There are also psalms that deliver words of wisdom, psalms that tell of God's greatness through His historic acts for His people, and psalms that glorify Jerusalem, or Zion, as God's dwelling place on earth. There are nine Acrostic psalms, where the verses start with the letters of the Hebrew alphabet in order; one of the Acrostic psalms, Psalm 119, has 22 eight-verse stanzas – one for each letter of the Hebrew alphabet.

Finally, there are two specific groups of psalms: the Imprecatory psalms, where the psalmist is calling for justice on the wicked or on Israel's enemies, and the Messianic psalms, which (often in the guise of praising Israel's current earthly king) look forward to the reign of the Messiah. For Christians, these Messianic psalms are prophetic in the extreme, with detailed descriptions of the life of Jesus and His coming Kingdom.

Despite this, the psalms are not grouped by any discernible themes; they are not ordered by date, author or subject. They also differ in style, in tone and indeed in length, from Psalm 119 with its 176 verses to Psalm 117 with just two. But they do all have two things in common: firstly, they are from the heart, and the psalmists who wrote them reflected all human emotions in their verses, and secondly, they are all, without exception, written in a very clear and easy-to-understand style. As such, they remain as meaningful today as when they were first written, a treasure chest to dip into and a source of inspiration for the faithful for over 3,000 years.

THE PSALMS

Psalm 1:
Two paths through life

Good morning. It is strange to be waking up on a Sunday – 15 March 2020 – and to be unable to go to church because of the corona crisis. So I have decided to start a daily habit of reading a psalm a day. I hope you will join me in this, and we can comment to each other as we do so.

We start with a psalm describing life's two roads: the life of the faithful person is contrasted with the life of wickedness and faithlessness. There is a balance to the psalm; the psalmist first differentiates the two types of people, the faithful and the wicked, through observation of their lives (verses 1-5), and then secondly by God's response (verse 6).

It is a short and simple psalm – we will meet far longer ones – and it is for me summarised in the last verse, verse 6: "For the Lord watches over the way of the righteous, but the way of the wicked will perish".

May the Lord watch over us in this crisis.

Sunday, 15 March 2020

This is the first Sunday that we have been told not to assemble at our church for the usual Sunday service. The virus has been getting closer, and already countries like Italy and Spain are in full lockdown, but the government is still publicly hoping to avoid having to impose such strict counter-measures here in the UK. But I don't think anybody really doubts what is coming.

For us it has also been a day of satisfaction and success, as our son Sam completed his move out of his old flat – the lease had expired – and we successfully moved most of his possessions into store and him back home to us.

For the house group that my wife Vicky and I belong to, and with whom we study the Bible, it is a break in our physical fellowship and mutual support for one another. Hence the suggestion that, through the psalms, we should continue to focus our thoughts together on the Lord in the extraordinary times we find ourselves.

Psalm 2: God's ultimate rule

Good morning, and thank you to those who responded to my invitation yesterday! Today we have a psalm celebrating God's total sovereignty over the world.

The author of this psalm is recorded as King David; it is the first of the psalms attributed to him, and we will meet many more. David knew about the challenges of kingship and how much (or how little) power even an absolute monarch really had – all earthly power is subject to the Sovereign Lord, and David knew that whatever the leaders of the world may think and try to do, however they try to break free from God (verse 3), it is all ineffective.

We are instead exhorted (verse 11) to "Serve the Lord with fear and rejoice with trembling" – an odd picture on the surface, but the fear here is more a sense of awe and reverence – and if we do, the psalmist promises (verse 12) "Blessed are all who take refuge in Him".

This psalm is one of the Messianic psalms, looking forward to the coming of Jesus. The reference in verse 2 to "the Lord and His anointed" can be taken to point to the earthly king of Israel, but it also and more meaningfully points to the Messiah and His reign – as the Israelites fully understood even 1,000 years before He came to earth.

For me, I shall be thinking how to "rejoice with trembling", given what looks like coming our way. What does it mean to you?

Monday, 16 March 2020

Today Sam's girlfriend Ellen came to spend a few days with us, and with them both having taken the day off in case Sam's move took longer than we expected, they have had time to settle in. We celebrated this evening by going out for dinner at a favourite steak restaurant; the restaurant, usually very busy even on a Monday night, was barely half full and already one could see that fewer people were going out, were on the streets.

We did not know it then but it was to be our last meal out for some time.

Psalm 3:
Calling on the Lord

Good morning. Today we have the first of what is known as the Petitioning psalms, where the psalmist, here once again David, calls on God for help, and expresses his confidence that God will hear his prayer and give him protection and peace.

This sequence of the psalmist describing his predicament to God (verses 1-2), declaring his confidence in God as his refuge and sure salvation (verses 3-6) and calling on God to act (verses 7-8) is one we will meet repeatedly in the psalms, especially those written by David. It shows a solid relationship between David and God, derived from much time spent in communion with Him, and a strong belief that his prayers would both be heard and answered.

It is not wrong to call on the Lord in times of difficulty, and we too can say with David (verse 7) "Arise O Lord! Deliver me, O Lord my God". Let us also have the confidence to add (verse 8) "From the Lord comes deliverance. May Your blessing be on Your people".

Amen to that!

Tuesday, 17 March 2020

This is the first day Sam has tried to work remotely through his laptop – his employer is still very much firing on all cylinders and has introduced WFH (working from home, an acronym we have all quickly become very familiar with!) for two days a week as an experiment.

The supermarkets are being besieged by people stocking up on essential supplies – pasta and tinned tomatoes appear to be the nation's favourite stand-by food, and toilet rolls have disappeared completely off the shelves. Chemists also report a run on thermometers, and none are to be had in any of the three pharmacies we usually go to.

Psalm 4:
Rejoicing in God's protection

Good morning. In Psalm 4, probably written as a pair with Psalm 3, which we looked at yesterday, the psalmist, once again David, continues his dialogue with God, both asking for help and expressing his confidence that God will not ignore his pleas.

It is traditional to consider Psalm 3 as a morning prayer, and Psalm 4 as more of an evening prayer (see verse 8, for example: "I will lie down and sleep in peace, for You alone, O Lord, make me dwell in safety"). The psalmist has thus "book ended" his day with prayer to the Lord.

I find the directness of David's approach to God in verse 1 striking: "Answer me when I call on You, O my righteous God. Give me relief from my distress, be merciful to me and hear my prayer". This is not the usual way one approaches asking something of someone powerful! It can only come from the psalmist's confidence that God will not reject the prayer, that God has promised to protect the faithful.

Do I have that confidence that God will hear my prayers too? Can we say with David (verse 8) "I will lie down and sleep in peace, for You alone, O Lord, make me dwell in safety"?

Wednesday, 18 March 2020

Ellen also tried working from Laburnum today, and I watched carefully to see if the home broadband stood up to two of them working hard on video conference calls. It did, fortunately.

Vicky is finding it more and more difficult to find basic food at the supermarket, not least as she is now having to stock the house for four people not two. Whole sections of the food aisles are completely bare. But local shops still seem fairly well stocked.

For my part, I had my annual "Well Man" blood test today. It was surreal going to the usually crowded surgery to find I was almost the only person there: all doctors' consultations have moved to telephone only wherever possible, but no-one has yet worked out how to take a blood sample via the internet!

Psalm 5: Defence against the lies of enemies

Good morning. What a wonderful psalm today, if you are still joining me in reading them each morning! From the opening two verses: "Give ear to my words O Lord, consider my sighing. Listen to my cry for help, my King and my God, for to You I pray", all the way to the end "For surely, O Lord, You bless the righteous; You surround them with Your favour as with a shield", this is a most apposite psalm in current times.

For me, the impact of the words "my King and my God" in verse 2 is especially striking. In the presence of the King we can make requests and wait in expectation for our God to answer. In the presence of the King our requests will never be selfish or outrageous but always acknowledging His glory. This is reverent fear of the Lord not the fear we see stalking our neighbourhoods today. We have everything to praise God for, we can show others His glorious good news as well and pray that they will come into his presence in the same "fearful" way.

And I particularly like verse 11: "But let all who take refuge in You be glad; let them ever sing for joy." I hold onto the fact that we can still be joyful in God whatever the circumstances – though I suspect it might prove a struggle in the coming weeks.

Let us pray to the Lord and ask Him to keep us safe in this crisis.

Thursday, 19 March 2020

The Government is ramping up its messaging to the nation, with a daily briefing at 5.00 pm and the incessant message "Stay at Home – Protect the NHS – Save Lives". It is a good message, and is playing well with people for whom belief in and support for the NHS is sacrosanct, in many ways in fact the closest that the country at large has to a religion.

Ellen returned to her flat today, to pick up enough clothes and other possessions for what might be an extended stay with us. Both public transport and the roads were noticeably less busy, she reported, but as yet the government is still resisting calls for a full lockdown. All up and down the High Street, though, restaurants are closing, and the daily death tolls are beginning to mount at an ever-increasing rate.

Psalm 6:
A prayer for deliverance

Good morning. Psalm 6 is another psalm of David, and is what commentators describe as a Penitential psalm, in which the psalmist pours out his woes to God and begs for His mercy.

David does not try to justify himself to God or claim that he does not deserve God's wrath. Indeed, in verses 1-7 he shows a measure of hopelessness and helplessness, because he knows that God's displeasure is fully justified. The only thing left to David is to call on the Lord to show mercy; until finally (verse 8-9) he knows that God has indeed heard his prayer, and will indeed answer it.

Given our circumstances, it would be so easy for us to focus on and worry about the challenges we are facing. What this psalm tells us is that despite his despair, David had his focus on the Lord. David is "worn out, tearful and sorrowful" (verses 6-7), but his focus on the Lord shows where his trust is.

Two points emerge for me: it is never possible to argue with God or claim we *deserve* better, but this does not stop us asking Him for mercy and, secondly, having done this, the psalm ends with the psalmist completely confident that the Lord will hear his prayer.

I shall certainly try to hold that confidence in these difficult times.

Friday, 20 March 2020

To my surprise the results of my blood test came back today, just two days after the blood sample had been taken. Usually it takes at least a week! The doctor rang me with the results, fortunately all clear and nothing to worry about.

The papers are full of concern at the prospect of a sunny weekend – the first real taste of spring for the year – and the natural desire of everyone to get out leading to mass gatherings of people. The big fear is that such gatherings are obvious places for the virus to be transmitted between people, and already all sport has moved behind doors, with games played in empty stadiums, or closed down completely.

For us this was the day we were meant to be going to Norway for a cruise on the Coastal Steamer. That was cancelled, of course – indeed, even if we wanted to go, Norway is no longer allowing foreigners into the country. All over Europe borders are closing, holidays are being cancelled, business is coming to a halt.

Psalm 7:
God the all-seeing Judge

Good morning. A longer psalm today, and most of it is about the psalmist's troubles with human enemies. David is assailed by Cush the Benjaminite, probably a henchman of Saul, but is confident of his innocence (verses 3-5), and asks the Lord to vindicate him and confirm his righteousness (verses 6-9). And this leads him to end the psalm with praise for God his defender.

For me, there is from this psalm and from David's words a clear message for our own lives in our current troubles. Verse 1 is surely applicable to us today: "O Lord my God, I take refuge in You; save and deliver me from all that pursues me".

Verse 9 again reminds us to look to the Lord for deliverance: "O righteous God, who searches minds and hearts, bring to an end the violence of the wicked and make the righteous secure". We cannot credit the virus with human emotions such as violence and wickedness, but we are assailed by it all the same, and can place our trust in the Lord to deliver us from it.

And the psalm ends with a verse of universal application: "I will give thanks to the Lord because of His righteousness, and will sing praise to the name of the Lord Most High".

This psalm encourages me to look through our challenges and work out how I can give thanks to the Lord.

Saturday, 21 March 2020

We are becoming increasingly concerned for the future of our local restaurants, many of them faithful friends for many years but almost all of them now closed. We have decided to keep giving them business through ordering take-aways where we can, and I spent the morning collecting take-away menus from those that were still operating.

Ellen has returned from her flat with everything she needs for an extended stay with us – already the government has urged the old and the vulnerable to stay at home and it is becoming more and more likely that they will extend this much wider in the near future.

Psalm 8: The majesty of God

Good morning. Psalm 8 returns us to the greatness of God, as the psalmist recalls God's majesty. Perhaps an appropriate psalm for us for a Sunday, after the woes and worries of the week.

The psalm also draws strength from God's purpose in creating man. God has created man for a purpose; the unspoken implication is that He will not abandon either that purpose or therefore mankind.

What comes to my mind is the children's song "My God is a great big God ... and He holds us in His hand". In its directness and simplicity, this psalm is giving us the same reassuring message.

The psalm ends with repeating the opening: "O Lord, our Lord, how majestic is Your name in all the earth". A message to be repeated with fervour, certainly. But also I think a challenge to us to see how we can make more people accept and understand it.

Sunday, 22 March 2020

Our local church has moved completely to online services by now, though at this stage the church building is not closed so the minister can lead a service in front of the altar, which gives a semblance of normality. But only a semblance, and the inability to meet really comes home as we miss the Sunday gathering with others of the congregation.

Today being a Sunday, we would usually have Vicky's father with us for Sunday lunch – he has been coming every Sunday for a number of years, and it is both good to see him and a chance for Vicky to check that he is in good health. Now alas he cannot come, as the government has ordered everyone over 70 (he is 85) to self isolate at home.

We also had the worrying news today that our nephew Nico, aged 21, has the virus and it is not a mild attack, as he is bed bound and increasingly short of breath. He has not been offered a hospital place so we pray he will pull through.

Psalm 9: Praise after the defeat of enemies

Good morning. After the joyous straightforwardness of yesterday's psalm we have a much more complex offering today. There is so much here that I am sure we will all find different bits to reflect on, different bits that resonate most for us.

For me, I pick out three elements of the psalm especially. First, verses 1 and 2, where the psalmist starts, as so often, with praise: "I will praise You, O Lord, with all my heart; I will tell of Your wonders. I will be glad and rejoice in You; I will sing praise to Your name, O Most High". What an antidote to the gloomy and worrying news all around us this is!

Next, I pick out verses 9 and 10. Here surely is another message tailored specifically for our troubled world: "The Lord is a refuge for the oppressed, a stronghold in times of trouble. Those who know Your name will trust in You, for You, O Lord, have never forsaken those who seek You". These are strong absolute words: a refuge, a stronghold, trust, never forsaken. Our God is not a fair-weather god who will fail us when we face difficulties.

And my last couplet to reflect especially on is verses 13 and 14: "O Lord, see how my enemies persecute me! Have mercy and lift me up from the gates of death, that I may declare Your praises in the gates of the Daughter of Zion and there rejoice in Your salvation".

Lift me up from the gates of death – we can all pray this at the moment. But the psalmist goes further; he asks for deliverance not for himself but "so that I may declare your praises". And did you see the lovely contrast between the gates of death and the gates of Jerusalem?

A wonderful reassuring psalm.

Monday, 23 March 2020

The weekend was as sunny, and the crowds at natural beauty spots as large, as the government had feared, leaving them with no choice but to announce the closure of all pubs, restaurants and non-essential shops, and to give 24 hours' notice of a dramatic lockdown. Not quite as severe as Italy's, but nothing like this has ever been announced by a British government in our history, not even in war-time.

Psalm 10:
Why do the wicked prosper?

Good morning. In many of the older Hebrew versions of the Old Testament, Psalm 10 is a continuation of Psalm 9. It is certainly a continuation of the psalmist's dialogue with God about why wicked people prosper, and where God is when His people are suffering. The theme of God being far away when needed most – as in our current times – is a recurrent one in Israel's history, and verse 1 expresses the psalmist's agonised doubts: "Why, Lord do You stand far off? Why do You hide Yourself in times of trouble?"

But instead of concluding that God is imaginary and does not really exist – or, which is almost worse, a fair-weather God who will abandon us when the going gets hard – in verse 10 the psalmist reiterates his plea for God to act: "Arise, Lord! Lift up Your hand, O God. Do not forget the helpless", and then in verse 14 his faith in God that He will indeed act: "But You, God, see the trouble of the afflicted; You consider their grief and take it in hand. The victims commit themselves to You; You are the helper of the fatherless".

And he closes, once again, in praise with verses 16-17: "The Lord is King for ever and ever; the nations will perish from His land. You, Lord, hear the desire of the afflicted; You encourage them, and You listen to their cry".

Like the psalmist, I will hold onto the fact that "the Lord is King for ever and ever", and that He "sees the trouble of the afflicted" and will "listen to their cry".

Tuesday, 24 March 2020

First my apologies for the lateness of today's Psalm Notes. Just about everyone I know arranged a conference call for this morning "because we know your diary is empty"! That, and to discuss the rapidly worsening situation facing the country as we enter the first day of lockdown, with all but essential workers told to stay at home.

Both Sam and Ellen are now therefore working completely from Laburnum for the foreseeable future. The home internet again stood up to the two of them, and even handled Vicky's regular bridge afternoons which she and her fellow enthusiasts have successfully moved online, but when I added my usage it became very slow! Vicky and I will have to restrain our use a bit I think, to ensure those working are not inconvenienced.

As someone pointed out, it is an ironic coincidence that the first day of the UK's lockdown was the 76th anniversary of the Great Escape, on 24 March 1944. Cue images of Steve McQueen on a motorbike ...

Psalm 11:
God's stability in a turbulent world

Good morning. Another shorter psalm today, with, for me, a simple and reassuring message.

From the opening of the psalm "In the Lord I take refuge" to the close "For the Lord is righteous, He loves justice; upright men will see His face", the psalmist declares his confidence that God reigns and His rule provides stability in a turbulent world.

And because of this, we should trust Him and if we do, we will be able to face our problems. The challenge I find is to hold to this even in the darkest times, which I suspect will increasingly be upon us.

Wednesday, 25 March 2020

Today is Sam's birthday and, since we cannot go out, we decided to have a take-away Chinese feast to celebrate. Alas our local Chinese take-away was in the process of closing up for the duration, though they very kindly agreed to fulfil our order for us. I gave them the order at about 2.00 pm, and went to pick it up as agreed at 7.00 pm. The shop was already very obviously no longer open, with "Closed" signs all over it, but they had completed our order, and it was quite delicious.

We are also delighted to hear that our nephew Nico has turned the corner and appears to be slowly on the mend. A response to prayer.

Psalm 12: The lies of the wicked

Good morning. At first glance, today's psalm seems of more general application than specifically relevant to our current situation. The psalmist is comparing the proud and false words of the people with the true and enduring words of God, and states his faith that the Lord will protect us from evil-sayers.

Verse 5b sums up the psalmist's faith: "I will now arise, says the Lord, I will protect them from those who malign them". And verse 7 reiterates this faith: "O Lord, You will keep us safe and protect us from such people for ever".

While this is a timeless truth that we can draw great comfort from, it seems to me also the case, with so much false news flying around on social media to worry us, that it is now more than ever necessary for me to focus on the Lord and His truth, which endures for ever.

Thursday, 26 March 2020

Social media is indeed exploding into action, with endless funny stories and pictures circulated and re circulated, and also, less happily, much false news and rumours being spread. Companies and newspapers that I barely know, or for whom I had written once five years ago, suddenly want to know my views on the economic crisis that is rapidly unfolding alongside the health crisis, and distant friends, who have dropped to the level of an annual Christmas card at most, suddenly feel it essential to ring up and spend 30 minutes on the phone. Far from having time on my hands, I am actually at the computer for more hours per day than since I left full-time work!

Sadly our hopes of supporting our local restaurants through take-aways is running into difficulties as more and more of them follow our local Chinese and decide it is too difficult or not worth their while to offer the service. A sad sign – I wonder how many will survive until the world re-opens.

Psalm 13:
Praying for relief from despair

Good morning. A short psalm today, but what a lot is packed into it.

The psalm has a familiar structure, with the psalmist first complaining to God, then petitioning Him for help, then declaring his confidence that God will act, and finally ending in praise. All in six verses!

For me, the most relevant verse for our current situation is verse 2: "How long must I wrestle with my thoughts and every day have sorrow in my heart?"

What I think the psalmist means here is that if we concentrate too much on our predicament, and endlessly churn over the news in our minds, we will drive ourselves to despair. The psalmist may not have had social media and coronavirus news 24/7, but he was well aware of the danger of obsessing over bad news. Instead, we should focus our minds on the Lord and His promise of salvation. And if we do we will, like the psalmist, "sing to the Lord, for He has been good to me".

Memo to self: concentrate on the Lord, not the news bulletins!

Friday, 27 March 2020

Today we learned that the Prime Minister, Boris Johnson, is suffering from the virus. It is a remarkable sign of how party politics has been suspended as largely irrelevant that across the political spectrum there has been genuine concern and good wishes for his recovery from all sides.

As if to prove my comment of yesterday, and an illustration of the explosion of communication that the lockdown has produced, and interest in the state of the nation, we held a Zoom* call for some of my cousins tonight, in which I was asked to lead a discussion on the economics of the coronavirus crisis and the consequences of the measures the government had imposed. I have to say it was largely the blind leading the blind! But it seemed to be appreciated and we have decided to repeat the Family Zoom roughly weekly.

** A simple-to-use video-conferencing system that the whole country rapidly became very proficient at!*

Psalm 14:
The fate of those who deny God

Good morning. How strange Saturday feels when it is not a special stay-at-home day after five busy days out on one's business.

Our psalm today has the theme "the safety of godliness, and the peril of ungodliness". The psalmist says that there are two types of people who reject God – the fool, who, despite all the evidence, denies God even exists, and the wicked or evil-doer, who knows of God's existence but chooses to ignore His rules.

The psalmist observes the actions of the wicked and how (verse 4) they prey upon God's people, but reiterates (verse 6) his confidence that the Lord will protect His people, and ends (verse 7) with a longing for the promised salvation of the Lord to come.

I am finding it striking as we go through the psalms each day how many of them start with fear, doubt and even anger, but end on an upbeat, with confidence in the Lord and praise for His righteousness and care for His people.

What a tonic that is, and I shall resolve to end each day, like the psalmist ends today's psalm, with the upbeat of concentrating on the Lord.

Saturday, 28 March 2020

As the lockdown gathers momentum, and looks ever more likely to last a considerable length of time, we begin receiving news of social and livery events being cancelled, and on our side the task starts of cancelling or rearranging holidays. Most people are being surprisingly good at returning deposits, but the cruise companies in particular face the complete destruction of their industry and are extremely keen that one rearranges for later rather than cancels completely.

But how much later will "later" need to be? How quickly will countries re-open their borders to foreigners, and trust that they will not thereby just reimport the virus? It is beginning to look like a very long haul indeed.

Psalm 15:
Advice on a righteous life with God

Good morning. I hope everyone has remembered to put their clocks forward!

In today's psalm, the psalmist ponders on guidelines for a God-centred life. It would be easy to read this as "*if* one lives one's life in this sinless way *then* one may live in God's sanctuary", and it is probably more the way the Old Testament Jews, living under the first Covenant, would have interpreted it.

But this ultimately is a frustrating, even depressing, reading, because no-one can live such a blameless life, and the logical conclusion is that no-one can hope to live with God.

For us, living in the period after Jesus had reset the Covenant and taken all our failings onto Himself, there is a different reading: "*if* we have accepted Jesus as Lord, *then* we will try to reflect this in the way we live our life".

We might say that under the Old Covenant a righteous life was a *preparation* for fellowship with God; under the New Covenant a righteous life is the *result* of fellowship with God, founded on faith.

As John says in his first epistle (1 John 1:6): "If we claim to have fellowship with God yet walk in the darkness, we lie and do not live by the truth".

So, albeit with slightly different logic underpinning my motives, I resolve that like the psalmist I should aim to live a righteous life as set out in this psalm.

Sunday, 29 March 2020

I think that the Church has been unwise to close so completely. At a time of national trauma, the sight of the National Church turning inward and invisible is not, I think, the right image to portray. And so different from other national crises when it was open to all and provided solace to many who might not otherwise have turned to it.

Psalm 16: The joy of a life of fellowship with God

Good morning. While in some psalms the psalmist is questioning, complaining, even despairing, this morning we have a psalm of pure joy. The psalmist reflects on the benefits and joy of a life lived in fellowship with God.

It is difficult to pick any particular part of this psalm out, because it is a flowing whole. From the opening verse: “Keep me safe, O God, for in You I take refuge” to the last: “You will fill me with joy in Your presence, with eternal pleasures at Your right hand”, the psalmist exudes confidence and the peace of mind of knowing that the Lord is in control and he will not be abandoned.

But perhaps in these worrying times I reflect especially on verses 8-10a: “I have set the Lord always before me. Because He is at my right hand I shall not be shaken. Therefore my heart is glad and my tongue rejoices; my body will also rest secure, because You will not abandon me to the grave”.

What a sentiment to start the week with. My challenge will be to put it into action!

Monday, 30 March 2020

The first week of the lockdown has seen news of the progress of the coronavirus getting increasingly grim. Though there is great public support for and thanks to the gallant staff of the NHS from our leaders, it is the shortages of PPE (personal protective equipment, another acronym we are all become familiar with very fast) and limited ability to conduct tests for the disease that characterises the government's handling of the crisis.

That, and the extraordinary amount of money the Treasury is making available to support the economy. The Treasury's expenditure could reach hundreds of billions of pounds – the biggest exercise in government support for the economy ever in peacetime. Truly a huge test of MMT, or Modern Monetary Theory (also known by its critics as the Magic Money Tree), and nobody knows how it will end or what the economy will look like in a year's time. But in reality, the Government probably has no alternative.

Psalm 17:
A plea for justice and protection

Good morning. In this morning's psalm, the psalmist calls on God with a plea for justice in the face of oppression and persecution.

The first part of the psalm, verses 1-6, reads very slightly oddly to us, as the psalmist seems to be trying to persuade God that he *deserves* God's protection because he has followed God's way of righteousness. We are, I think, back in the mindset of Psalm 15 from two days ago, where under the Old Covenant a righteous life was the precondition for fellowship with God. Whereas we who live under the New Covenant can be assured of our ability to call upon God because we have accepted Jesus as Lord and can therefore receive God's grace.

But thereafter the psalm is more straightforward, a declaration of confidence by the psalmist that God will protect him. The heart of this statement of confidence is verses 6-9:

"I call on You, my God, for You will answer me; turn Your ear to me and hear my prayer. Show me the wonders of your great love, You who save by Your right hand those who take refuge in You from their foes. Keep me as the apple of Your eye; hide me in the shadow of Your wings from the wicked who are out to destroy me, from my mortal enemies who surround me".

What a wonderful thing for the psalmist to be able to say this. What a joy that we too can say this with true assurance that God will not fail us.

Tuesday, 31 March 2020

It is interesting to see how different sectors of the economy are responding to the crisis. For once the accolade of "most completely missing the public mood" has not been won by the banking sector, despite the fact that they are still charging 39.9% for personal overdrafts despite the Bank of England lowering their base rate to an unprecedented 0.1% ... Step forward Premier League footballers, who are grossly, perhaps obscenely, overpaid at the best of times, but whose union argues that they should not take a pay cut to enable their hard-pressed clubs to weather the storm, "because it would result in them paying less tax to the Exchequer at this difficult time". "Tin ear" does not even begin to describe it!

Psalm 18:
Gratitude for deliverance and victory

Good morning. Today we come across the first of the really long psalms in the Bible; at 50 verses, Psalm 18 is the fourth longest in the book. Tempting as it might be to break it up into more than one day's study, if one reads through it as a whole (and, after all, we all have time to do so!) one is rewarded with a magnificent hymn of praise that will roll round your head for a long time after you have finished reading it.

The psalmist is David, and it is thought that he wrote this psalm towards the end of his life, reflecting back and recognising God's hand in everything that had happened to him and that he had been able to achieve. (The psalm is almost identical to his song in 2 Samuel 22). It starts with a bang – David certainly knows how to grab the listener's attention – with the declaration: "I love You, O Lord, my strength. The Lord is my rock, my fortress and my deliverer", and from there on it is a song of gratitude for deliverance and victory against all the many enemies David had faced in his life.

For me, it is difficult and perhaps, with such a long psalm, even slightly counterproductive to go through it verse by verse. The whole point of the psalm seems to me to be its cumulative effect as the repetitions – of God's goodness, His strength, His care for David, and of David's feeling of security in God's hands and thanks and praise for His love – roll on and on until David has no possible response except verse 49: "Therefore I will praise You among the nations, O Lord; I will sing praises to Your name".

But if I am to pick out just one verse for us in these strange times, my choice might be verse 46: "The Lord lives! Praise be to my Rock! Exalted be God my Saviour". What a truth to hang onto – the Lord does live, He is our Saviour, and will not abandon us. I will certainly be concentrating on that today.

Wednesday, 1 April 2020

The supermarkets are stabilising at last after the run on essentials in the first week of the lockdown. They have improved their supplies and their shelf-stackers are performing heroically to keep the shelves from looking bare. In addition, they have all introduced queueing systems to ensure not too many people are in the shop at one time, and the net result is fuller shelves and less panic buying. A great relief.

Psalm 19:
God's creation reveals His greatness

Good morning. Today's psalm has a calmer feel to it after those of recent days. Gone are the pleas for help in times of difficulties, gone are the repeated statements of confidence in the Lord, which one sensed were as much as anything so that the psalmist could quell his own doubts and fears.

Instead we have a lovely poem in which the psalmist declares that both God's creation and His Word reveal His greatness.

I find it interesting that the psalmist dwells longer on God's *law* as evidence of His majesty than on His creation. Both are remarkable, but only those who have lived in a lawless land will know the true value of just laws, justly applied.

Note also that whereas we tend to think of laws as restricting, as denying us freedom, the psalmist is clear that God's laws revive us (verse 7), give us joy (verse 8), are more precious than gold (verse 10).

By the end of this psalm the psalmist is overcome by the greatness of God, and he closes with words that are so familiar to us, as many preachers use them to open their sermons:

"May the words of my mouth and the meditations of my heart be pleasing in your sight, O Lord my Rock and my Redeemer".

Amen to this!

Thursday, 2 April 2020

The good weather and clear skies are quite a talking point. Pollution is noticeably reduced and the skies are so much clearer with 90% of aeroplanes grounded and the roads with well under 50% of their usual traffic. Our lawns are growing fast in the spring sunshine and I have unleashed my trusty (and rather ancient) electric mower – not much used in recent years as we have been employing professional gardeners. Fortunately it still works; unfortunately it is still the rather cheap and inadequate electric mower it always was!

Psalm 20:
A prayer for victory in battle

Good morning. This morning we have a slightly different psalm: although it is marked as "A psalm of David", it is mainly a prayer not *by* David but by the people *for* David – the "you" in verses 1-5 is singular.

The psalm is a prayer for victory in battle. The people pray for their king's success (verses 1-5), and the king responds with his confidence that the Lord will answer their prayer and protect him (verses 6-8).

But on another level the whole psalm is deeply prophetic, and looks forward to Jesus and his battle against death, sin and the devil. With this interpretation verse 5a takes on new meaning for us as Christians: "We will shout for joy when you are victorious and will lift up our banners in the name of our God".

With Easter just nine days away we can all look forward to shouting for joy at Jesus's victory.

In the meantime, I shall hold on to verse 7: "Some trust in chariots and some in horses, but we trust in the name of the Lord our God"; and verse 9, the cry of Christians down the ages: "O Lord ... answer us when we call!"

Friday, 3 April 2020

Alongside our gardeners being unable to call, our cleaning lady is also no longer coming round. And with Vicky shouldering the main burden of shopping and catering for the household, I have taken on the cleaning, ironing, hoovering and the like. Not that there is very much ironing; since none of us is going into town any more, or even much out of the house, there is no grime on our clothes worth speaking of and things like shirts and trousers can be worn for rather longer before they get too grubby. It really is a striking demonstration of how polluted our city air usually is.

A fascinating Family Zoom (see 28 March) today, led by one of my cousins who lives in Saudi Arabia and works at our embassy in Riyadh. He was trying to explain Saudi Arabia to us – he titled his talk "A complicated friend" – but I am afraid to say that even after listening to him my view of the country remains unchanged: it is for me a difficult place, an example of how a false faith, sternly imposed, can twist society, and it is the one country of the well over 100 that I have visited that I would not willingly return to.

Psalm 21:
Praise after victory has been won

Good morning. Our psalm this morning can be seen as a continuation of psalm 20. The victory prayed for in yesterday's psalm seems to have been won, and now the psalmist is thanking God and acknowledging that it is from Him that all blessings flow.

The whole psalm, especially verses 1-7, is also deeply messianic, looking forward to Jesus's victory. Indeed, one commentary suggests that the original Hebrew word translated as king in verse 1 overtly referred to the Messiah.

Whether we read the psalm as such, or in the more literal sense with the king identified as David, it is a powerful reminder that when God answers our prayers and gives us what we desire, we must quickly and openly thank and praise Him. As the last verse says: "Be exalted, O Lord, in your strength; we will sing and praise Your might".

Saturday, 4 April 2020

So ends a week in which the twin crises, health and economic, have competed with each other to deliver the most gloomy news. The death tolls from the virus continue to mount, at what is still an accelerating rate, but all the talk is of the economic crisis, which threatens to be worse than any recession since the Great Depression, and possibly worse even than that.

And as well as the economic damage, which will affect everyone, crashing economies do also cost lives – lives lost because people cannot access (or in some countries afford) health services, lives lost to default and debt, lives lost to despair. When countries' GDPs shrink, so do their life expectancy rates. We may yet end up with more deaths caused by the recession brought on to fight COVID-19 than from the disease itself.

But a break from all that today – well it is the weekend – as the BBC decided to re-show some of the great Rugby League challenge cup finals of the last 50 years. Very enjoyable, and an opportunity to hear once again, after 35 years, the totally inimitable voice of Eddie Waring, probably the best known commentator of a minor sport the BBC has ever had – his fame extended far beyond those who followed the game!

Psalm 22:
From great suffering to great joy

Good morning, on a glorious Palm Sunday. And we have one of the truly great Messianic psalms today. The entirety of the first 21 verses points directly to Jesus and His suffering on the cross, from the opening cry of anguish, so familiar to all of us, to the detailed description of the crucifixion.

The psalm is a prayer that carries the psalmist from great suffering to great joy. Despite rejection by his friends and apparent rejection by God, he continues to believe that God will rescue him from his difficulties, and he looks forward to praising God publicly (verse 22: "I will declare your name to my brothers, in the congregation I will praise You") when he has been restored to good fortune. And the psalm closes with the psalmist looking forward with confidence to the day when God will rule over the entire earth.

It is clear that for the psalmist – as for Jesus on the cross – it is rejection by God, or the feeling of being forsaken, that causes the greatest anguish. It is not for nothing that the adjective *God-forsaken* has such awful overtones of absolute despair. All things are bearable, even our current crisis, if we believe God is with us; but the person without God is truly lost and defenceless.

I find it remarkable that when the psalmist wrote these words, he had neither seen nor heard of crucifixion as a method of execution, let alone the Roman customs surrounding it – yet the first two-thirds of the psalm reads almost like an eye-witness account of Jesus's suffering. If you are short of things to do in the lockdown, count how many of the phrases in verses 1-21 can be found to have exact parallels in actual events recorded in the gospel accounts of Jesus's crucifixion. I counted at least a dozen – and they are all worth meditating on.

Sunday, 5 April 2020

Indeed the weather has been glorious for the last few days, and today has been no exception – we had Sunday lunch in the garden on the patio. The garden is a great release in the lockdown, and we are very much blessed to have it; and how lucky we are in one sense that the crisis has occurred now not in, say, November, when the weather was poor and the days short.

One consequence of the dry weather and sunshine is that the lawns are very dry, especially the front lawn, which, being raised up, always struggles to retain moisture. So we have been running the sprinklers on it. I do not recall ever doing that before Easter in previous years.

Psalm 23:
The Lord is my shepherd

Good morning. Today we reach Psalm 23, perhaps the best known and best loved of all the psalms. And however well one knows it, what a joy it is to read it again.

In six short verses the psalmist extols God as our protector, provider, guide and comforter. The image of the shepherd is so powerful that Jesus himself used it to describe how He looked after God's people (most clearly in John's gospel, chapter 10), and it has remained a favourite image of Jesus for Christians ever since.

The last two verses portray a slightly different picture, this time of the Lord as our host. Again, this is a very powerful image as, in the culture of ancient Israel, a host was responsible not only for feeding his guests but also protecting them and ensuring their general wellbeing. To "dwell in the house of the Lord for ever", therefore, was to enjoy the privilege of God's bounty and protection for ever.

All of the psalm is a great joy to the believer. But perhaps in current days, verse 4 has special resonance: "Even though I walk in the valley of the shadow of death, I will fear no evil, for You are with me: Your rod and Your staff, they comfort me".

A personal challenge – can I repeat this as fervently as the psalmist? Do I feel comforted, even in "the valley of the shadow of death"?

Monday, 6 April 2020

We have failed to find anyone to repair our conservatory – the gutter leaks, and one of the panes of glass on the roof has slipped and may not be entirely waterproof any more in heavy rain. But ringing and emailing no less than three local conservatory maintenance companies elicited not even a single response, far less an offer to come out to help us. When the crisis is over we will no doubt have the opposite problem: such a backlog of work needing doing that tradesmen will be unavailable for months!

Leaking gutters I can try to fix, though, so, recalling all of my rusty handyman skills, I climb the ladder and try to seal the hole. Knowing whether it has been effective will have to wait until we next have rain, of which there is no sign at all in the forecasts.

Psalm 24:
God the glorious and eternal King

Good morning. Today's psalm is in three parts, which together sum up how the psalmist wanted God's people to live.

The first part (verses 1 and 2) declares the greatness of God, the creator of everything – not just the earth, but all who live in it.

The second part (verses 3-6) expands on this and speaks of how mankind can come into a relationship with this great Creator-God. "Clean hands and a pure heart", as verse 4 puts it, are required, in other words both God-focused deeds and thoughts.

And finally the third section (verses 7-10) declares twice that God, the King of Glory, will be welcomed into union with His people. It is thought that these verses may have been used at the temple in Jerusalem, with the people declaring that their God was with them and among them.

The psalm reaffirms three great truths: the greatness of God, the fact that even so He welcomes us to come into His presence and, even more, that He wants to be in our presence. For me it is a wonderful thing, worthy of both prayer and praise, that so all-powerful a God wants us to be part of His kingdom, to share in His glory.

Tuesday, 7 April 2020

A great treat today as we tried my home-cured bacon. We have tried a number of home kits for food over the years: homemade sausages are tremendous (and great fun to make using the sausage-making machine), and home cured salmon has also been extremely successful, though the homemade cheese was nothing like so memorable and not worth repeating. But this was the first time we have tried making bacon. And boy was it good – possibly the best of the lot! We made a big pack, but it all went in under 48 hours ...

Today it was announced that the Prime Minister, who was declared to have the virus 11 days ago, has not recovered and has been moved to hospital and then fairly swiftly into intensive care. The government statements are upbeat and the PM himself is said to be his usual ebullient and confident self; but this is one problem that his usual gung-ho approach to life may not be able to solve.

Psalm 25: A prayer for guidance and pardon

Good morning. Today we have another psalm where the psalmist is appealing to God from a position of difficulty. By some counts nearly half of the 150 psalms in the Bible mention the psalmist's enemies, whether physical oppressors or the more subtle enemies of sin, temptation and the devil.

Psalm 25 is a very personal prayer; it is for the most part in the first person singular, a direct appeal to God. The psalmist seeks protection (verses 1-3), guidance (verses 4 and 5), pardon (verses 6 and 7), and more guidance (verses 8-15), before returning to his opening plea for protection (verses 16-21).

It is only in the last verse, after this litany of personal requests, that the psalmist widens his prayer to include all of Israel in his plea for redemption.

I find that there is much to reflect on in this psalm. For me, the verses that resonate most are verses 4 and 5: "Show me Your ways, O Lord, teach me Your paths, guide me in Your truths and teach me, for You are my God and Saviour, and my hope is in You all day long".

To really build a fellowship with God we need His guidance and help. What a great joy that we are able to ask Him for it, with the confidence that our request will be heard.

Wednesday, 8 April 2020

One feature of the lockdown has been how comparatively seamlessly activity has moved to the internet. Working from home, ordering things online, and Zoom conference calls have all made life much less impossible than if this crisis had hit even, say, 30 years ago. I ripped my pyjamas at the end of last week; the replacement pair (ordered online) arrived from John Lewis today, just five days later.

But this does rely on the IT working! And my email engine, Outlook, has fallen over and is no longer properly behaving. I try to suppress the vague feeling of panic – it is when modern technology stops working that one realises how totally one relies on it – and attempt to fix it. No joy at all, but fortunately I know a techie who can. And, even more fortunately, he can do it remotely by connecting to my laptop over the self-same internet.

Two hours later and we are all good to go again. And, breathe …

A very good family Zoom call tonight, with both daughters and their other halves joining the four of us here at Laburnum for a pub quiz. The younger generation are very kind with their questions – not too much modern culture – and Vicky and I end up the victors. I suspect they won't be so generous to us next time!

Psalm 26: Commitment to God

Good morning. In today's psalm the psalmist, usually thought to be David, declares his loyalty to God and willingness to stand up to examination of his faith.

It is an interesting psalm that at times reads almost as if the psalmist is boasting of his good works. But David's confidence is, in fact, based on his life of faith – verse 1b, "I have trusted in the Lord without wavering", and verse 3, "For Your love is ever before me, and I walk continually in Your truth".

And this in turn gives David the desire not just to walk with God in private but to proclaim his faith publicly – verse 7, "proclaiming aloud Your praise and telling of Your wonderful deeds", and verse 12, "in the great assembly I will praise the Lord".

It is a psalm of someone of deep and unshakeable faith. And it leads me to ask myself how I can deepen my faith to approach that of the psalmist's.

Thursday, 9 April 2020

Today I learned of the death of a good friend, a former Bank of England and Political Economy Club colleague, from the virus. He was 73 and in mixed health but it is still a shock, and brings things closer to home. The worst feature is that we are not able to go to his funeral or hold a memorial service. There will be one, I am sure, in due course, but months and months away no doubt. Will we go through a period with multiple memorial services every month as we all catch up?

Psalm 27:
Unwavering confidence in God's blessings

Good morning, and greetings to all on this Good Friday morning. Our psalm today is one of unwavering confidence in and desire for God.

The psalmist – assumed to be David – starts with a ringing statement of faith, and the first verse sets the tone for the whole psalm and indeed David's entire life: "The Lord is my light and my salvation – whom shall I fear? The Lord is the stronghold of my life – of whom shall I be afraid?"

What a wonderful sentiment for us too, not least in these strange times. And, interestingly, while we are of course very familiar with Jesus being called the Light of the World, it is one of the few places in the Old Testament that the attribute Light is given to God Himself.

With his great faith, David wanted nothing more than to be in God's presence, for God to hear his prayer, and the heart of the psalm (verses 4-12) is a petition for this communion with God. It reminds us that the most painful moments for a Christian are not when God is angry with us – His wrath is fully justified – but when He seems to abandon or reject us.

Hence the urgent prayer in verse 9: "Do not hide Your face from me, do not turn Your servant away in anger; You have been my helper. Do not reject me or forsake me, God my Saviour". The directness of the language here – "Do not …" – is striking; this is a desperate plea.

But, as so often, the psalm ends on an upbeat, as if by praying the psalm the psalmist has allayed and soothed his concerns, and the final two verses return to the confidence of the opening: "I remain confident of this: I will see the goodness of the Lord in the land of the living. Wait for the Lord; be strong and take heart and wait for the Lord". What a statement of faith – is it one I can also make?

Friday, 10 April 2020

Another lovely day, and we celebrated with the first barbecue of the year. Sam made a stunning focaccia, and we had Greek souvlaki, dips and salad. And a couple of bottles of Mavrotragano from Santorini, and cheese and a Quinta de Vesuvio 1995 port to close. Life is still good, despite our troubles.

Psalm 28:
Calling on God for help

Good morning. Today's psalm is another that is ascribed to David, and it follows the pattern of several we have already seen.

The psalm opens with a plea to God to be heard (verses 1 and 2) and, equally important for the psalmist, for God to respond. David had confidence that God would indeed hear his prayer, but he was still keen to have a sign from God to reassure him that he was being listened to.

The main prayer in the psalm then follows in verses 3-5, as the psalmist asks to be spared the fate of the wicked.

Finally in this short psalm David ends, as he does so often, in praise and thanks – thanks that his personal prayer has been heard and answered, and praising the Lord who is the strength of His people.

It is remarkable how, in this series of psalms, David finds so many different ways to express these fundamental feelings. I note particularly in today's psalm the difference between the hearts of the wicked, which harbour malice (verse 3), and the heart of a believer, which contains trust in the Lord and great joy (verse 7).

Saturday, 11 April 2020

The Prime Minister has been released from intensive care and, while not yet fully recovered, is, one assumes, considered to be no longer in danger. The sense of relief in the nation is tangible and I think genuine: this is not just the natural pleasure at an individual's survival, or the equally understandable relief that we have avoided the distraction of a leadership election at a time of great national stress, but also a sign that he is genuinely popular, and not just among his supporters. His relentlessly upbeat optimistic approach to life and his can-do ebullience may not be to everyone's taste or the answer to all problems, but it is surely better in these difficult times than the caution and hang-dog misery of his predecessor!

Johnson responds with a heartfelt and very emotional message of thanks and praise for the NHS and the care he has received. If anyone else had tried it, it would be thought mawkish, but he carried it off well. It will be interesting to see how much of the current adulation of the NHS survives this crisis and is carried forward into practical support.

Psalm 29:
A hymn of praise

Good morning, on this strange but still joyous Easter morning.

And what a psalm we have for Easter Day. There are no doubts, no second thoughts, no requests or pleas to God in this psalm – it is one long hymn of praise and worship. For Jews, it has a special resonance, as it is the psalm sung as the scrolls are returned to where they are stored after having been read on the Sabbath.

The opening two verses, in which we are all called to "worship the Lord in the splendour of His holiness", give way to a recital of His great power and majesty. Here the Hebrew poetic technique of repetition for emphasis is used again and again; the Lord's name is invoked no less than 18 times in this short psalm, and the "voice of the Lord" seven times. This might be a wonderful psalm to re read in a violent thunderstorm!

Finally, after the energetic activity of the heart of the psalm, we reach the calmer waters of the close, and the last two verses declare that "the Lord is enthroned as King for ever" and "the Lord blesses His people with peace".

What a wonderful psalm for Easter Day, and for all time.

Sunday, 12 April 2020

More domestic drama today as water from the bath starts to come through the ceiling of my study below! And once again one realises that lockdown is OK and survivable just until something goes wrong that requires someone to come out and fix it – which they can't.

We empty the bath and mop up my study – fortunately I caught it quite early and there is no lasting damage, just water stains on the ceiling and a few damp books. But we cannot use that bathroom while everything dries out. Fortunately we have the "first world solution" of simply using the other bathroom for all four of us for the moment!

Psalm 30:
A psalm of celebration

Good morning. Today's psalm is another psalm of David, and has an unusual heading: "For the dedication of the temple". It was thus to be sung at a happy and celebratory event, and reminds us that although many of David's greatest psalms were cries to the Lord from a position of difficulty or danger, he did not neglect to sing to the Lord in the good times as well.

The psalm is a celebration of God's deliverance and faithfulness. David acknowledges that there have been and will always be times when God is angry with His faithful, but they are short, and God's grace lasts for ever and will endure. As verse 5 puts it: "For His anger lasts only a moment, but His favour lasts a lifetime; weeping may remain for a night, but rejoicing comes in the morning".

And again, in verse 11: "You turned my wailing into dancing; You removed my sackcloth and clothed me with joy, that my heart may sing to You and not be silent. O Lord my God, I will give You thanks for ever".

The message I will take away from this glorious psalm is that however challenging our present circumstances are, I should remember with David that God will indeed in time turn our wailing into dancing, and clothe us with joy.

Monday, 13 April 2020

My study has dried in the atypically warm April weather, and we tentatively try to find the source of the leak. It appears to be the overflow pipe on the bath, and the main drain still seems sound so, while baths are out till we can get a plumber, showers are OK. Much relief all round, as pressure on the second bathroom would have been intense with four of us in the house.

A glorious long Easter weekend comes to a close with the fourth consecutive dry warm day. The police are getting more and more agitated at the numbers of people congregating in parks and beauty spots and breaking the social distancing guidelines – the rules of the lockdown do allow one to leave the house once a day for exercise (as well as for essential food or medicine shopping, or to go to work for key workers), but it is not clear how this is to be enforced and there are many stories in the press of over-officious policemen confronting people. One hopes sense will prevail – the lockdown will only work if most people tolerate the restrictions on our freedoms, and they will only continue to tolerate them if they seem reasonable and justified.

Psalm 31:
Trust in the Lord

Good morning. Today's psalm returns us to times of stress, and focuses us on the need for absolute commitment to God when we are facing difficulties. There are no half measures in the psalm, from its length and frequent use of the Hebrew style of repetition for emphasis to the characterisation of God as the psalmist's refuge, a deeply significant word in a world where physical dangers dominated (the word occurs four times, three of them in the first four verses). But just as insistent as the psalmist's prayers for God's protection (verses 1-13) is his confidence and trust that God will answer those prayers (verses 14-18), and his determination to praise the Lord for doing so (verses 19-24).

What a model for life this is, especially in a time of difficulty: turn to the Lord in difficulties, rely on Him completely, praise Him for His goodness in protecting us.

The psalm clearly resonated deeply with the Jews, and is often quoted elsewhere in other passages of Scripture – most famously, of course, Jesus's last words on the cross were verse 5: "Into your hands I commit my spirit". Stephen the Martyr also used these words when he was stoned to death (Acts 7:59).

The psalm was also credited by Martin Luther as the spark that started him thinking afresh about his faith. Luther relates that he was initially deeply troubled by verse 1b: "deliver me in Your righteousness". How could God's righteousness deliver him? The righteousness of God – His great justice – could only condemn him to hell as a righteous punishment for his sins. Luther finally realised what the righteousness of God revealed by the gospel is. It is not speaking of the holy righteousness of God that condemns the guilty sinner, but of the God-gift of righteousness that is given to the sinner who puts his trust in Jesus. Luther said of this experience: "I grasped the truth that the righteousness of God is that righteousness whereby, through grace and sheer mercy, He justifies us by faith. Therefore I felt myself to be reborn and to have gone through open doors into paradise".

Let us with Luther pray to God: "Deliver me in Your righteousness", and say with the psalmist verses 14-15: "But I trust in You, O Lord; I say 'You are my God'. My times are in Your hand, deliver me from my enemies". And we too will then be able to echo the psalm's final verse: "Be strong and take heart, all you who hope in the Lord".

Tuesday, 14 April 2020

And with today's psalm, we have completed the first full month of our travel through psalms. "Normal" seems a long time ago.

It is a day of yet more domestic drama, as Vicky's car breaks down – or rather, simply won't start – as she tries to come home from delivering food and other shopping to her father 25 miles away. A totally flat battery, gone without any warning or previous loss of power at all.

Fortunately I have a breakdown cover service. Even more fortunately, they are working. Better still, they know of a garage near Vicky's father who are also working and will come out to her. They diagnose a dead battery, not just flat but totally dead, and direct her to a nearby Kwik-Fit station that is open and agrees to sell her a new one and install it. And after a very worrying couple of hours she is on her way home.

But once again one is left realising how fragile modern life can be and how much one relies on things working – or people being available when one needs them put right.

Psalm 32: The blessing of forgiveness

Good morning. This morning we have a psalm of penitence, but also of a forgiven person rejoicing in the wonder of the grace of God. For the psalmist, sin is dealt with, sorrow is comforted, ignorance is instructed.

Few things in childhood match the worry of wondering if your parents will find out when you have done something wrong. Should you own up and risk punishment, or try to hide it? In the end, telling them is always the best way: you may be punished, but you will end the greater punishment of worry.

So it is, the psalmist declares, with God – only more so because God always knows what we have done. He longs to forgive us, to guide us in His ways – but we must come to Him in penitence first.

A simple theme but one of the great truths of our life with God: the joy of forgiveness, of a relationship restored. I love this second element, and the fact that the psalm is all about a relationship between us and God: I'll listen to you (verses 1-7) and you listen to me (verses 8-10) and we'll rejoice and sing (verse 11).

This was said to be St Augustine's favourite psalm; he had it written on the wall by his bed so he could meditate on it better.

Wednesday, 15 April 2020

We are beginning to wonder whether there is a theme to recent days, as yet another thing goes wrong with no warning. This time it is Vicky's laptop, which refuses to connect to the house wi-fi internet (though it can see it), and thus won't let her join her thrice-weekly online bridge with her bridge circle.

Forget leaking baths and water through the ceiling, or car breakdowns 25 miles from home – this is serious! I struggle with the laptop for 10 minutes, poking at things I don't fully understand and clicking random buttons, and suddenly it seems to work again. I have no idea what was wrong or what I did to put it right. But we live to fight another day.

The weather is finally turning a bit cooler, though the lawns will take a further cut after all the recent sun and need more watering.

Psalm 33:
Praise to the Creator God

Good morning. After yesterday's penitence we move today to praise, with the psalmist declaring God worthy of our worship because He is our Creator, our Defender and our Saviour, and because His Word is righteous and constant.

The psalm is a call to *communal* praise, with the "you" in the first verse being plural, and places emphasis on music – singing, and the playing of the harp and lyre. Let us all look forward to the day when we can join together again in communal praise!

The psalm also highlights one of the features of the Book of Psalms: how varied they are. Psalms of penitence and psalms calling for God's help in times of stress are interspersed with psalms of praise, and quiet psalms of personal reflection and prayer with joyful ones of communal worship. This certainly makes our daily journey through the book more interesting and revealing, and also accurately mirrors our human life, which is neither all sorrow nor all plain sailing.

The one constant, running through all the psalms we have read so far, is a recognition of the greatness of God. It is an inspiration to me to make it also the one constant running through my life as well.

Thursday, 16 April 2020

The litany of domestic disasters continues – today there is no hot water as the boilers shut off overnight. Fortunately we can see the problem (low water pressure) and, courtesy of asking the plumber to fix a new water injection pipe only a couple of months ago, the solution is very easy to arrange. Serendipity, but again it reminds one of the fragility of much of modern life and how close one runs to major inconvenience.

After mending the boilers, to the post office – it is still working, and we have a parcel to send to our daughter in Royston. It is strangely empty though; only two counters open of the usual six, and no queue for service.

The main news today is the increasing talk of when and how the government will end, or at least ease, the lockdown. The problem they have is that the twin crises are intertwined. And the solution to the health crisis – lockdown, self-isolation and social distancing – is creating the second, the economic crisis. At some point we will have to get the economy going again. But when? Do it too soon, and the virus will roar back; do it too late, and the economic damage may be beyond easy repair.

So far the government seems to be in the Red Queen camp of "Jam tomorrow". A week ago they warned that it would be "at least three weeks" and yesterday the message was unchanged – "at least three weeks".

Psalm 34: Reliance on the Lord at all times

Good morning. In today's psalm we see David once more in difficulties, and he responds by once more expressing his complete trust in and reliance on the Lord.

The triumph and joy in this song is so clear that it is easy to forget the context. David was on the run – a fugitive from Saul – and it is thought that he wrote the psalm while hiding in a cave after failing to find refuge in the Philistine city of Gath (the story is in 1 Samuel 21:10-22:1). Even for David this was a notable low-point, yet his thoughts turned to God and praise even so. For any of us facing a low-point in our lives, this can serve as a great example and inspiration!

I note how the psalm starts (verse 1) with "I will extol the Lord at all times". Praise is not just for the good times, nor prayer reserved only for times of trial. And David does praise the Lord, in abundant terms, and invites us to do so too. Much of the first part of the psalm is an exhortation to join with David in praising God, for example verse 3: "Glorify the Lord with me, let us exalt His name together"; verse 8: "Taste and see that the Lord is good"; verse 11: "Come, my children, listen to me; I will teach you the fear of the Lord".

Verses 9 and 10, "Fear the Lord, you his saints, for those who fear Him lack nothing. The lions may grow weak and hungry, but those who seek the Lord lack no good thing", have been seen by some as justification for the "prosperity gospel". But God distinguishes between what we want and what we need. It is an important distinction in times of trial such as now: what we may want is for the threat of disease to end and normality to return, but what we need is to trust that God will bring this about when the time is right for His purposes.

And then we will be able to see with David that, in the words of the psalm's closing verse, "The Lord redeems His servants; no one will be condemned who takes refuge in Him".

Friday, 17 April 2020

A quieter day for a change – no domestic disasters! And the weather has broken with some rain, the first in April (and we are more than half way through the month). Not really enough, but the garden has certainly welcomed it.

Psalm 35:
A prayer for help against one's enemies

Good morning. Today we have one of what are commonly known as the Imprecatory psalms, where the psalmist asks God, often in strong terms, to defeat and destroy the enemies of His people.

These psalms can read quite harshly, almost vindictively, and today's is no exception. But behind the aggressive language there is a more godly theme to the psalm. The psalmist, in this case David, is asking for three things:

Firstly, *protection and reassurance*, as in verse 2b "come to my aid", and verse 3b "Say to my soul, I am your salvation".

Secondly, *deliverance, and that God's righteous justice be done*. This is the sense of verse 24 at the end of the long prayer for David's enemies to suffer: "Vindicate me in Your righteousness, O Lord my God".

And thirdly, that *justice be seen to be done, so that God's people may praise Him*, as so often David ends the psalm praising the Lord. In the words of verse 28: "My tongue will speak of Your righteousness and of Your praises all day long".

David had complete faith in the Lord; he did not take matters into his own hands but allowed God to act, knowing firstly that He would indeed provide a sure protection, and secondly that this would further glorify God in the eyes of His people.

I too should trust in the Lord, and allow Him to act.

Saturday, 18 April 2020

Rain overnight, more substantial this time. I am relieved of the duty of running the sprinklers on the lawn.

The Post Office is keeping going, but clearly struggling. We learn that none of the cards we sent the family for Easter – first class and posted four days before – arrived on time, and some took over a week.

Sam has cooked dinner tonight, a feast, and we dress up smart for it. I have a jacket and tie on. I realise I have not worn a tie for over five weeks; it took a while to remember how to tie it! We end the meal with a bottle of Californian Black Muscat, a sweet red wine and definitely a first for both Sam and Ellen. It is quite delicious.

Psalm 36:
A contemplation on God

Good morning. Today we have another psalm of David, this time a more contemplative one. For once David does not seem to be in great danger or distress, and instead of urgent prayers for help and protection, he is able to reflect more on the nature of God.

The psalm does this by contrasting the sinful lives of the wicked, who ignore and do not fear God, with God's faithfulness, justice and love. I am struck by the way David struggles to find ways of describing the magnitude of God's love in verses 5 and 6; he is clearly thinking of the biggest things he can to compare it to.

Verse 9 also paints the image of God as the Fountain of Life. We are of course so familiar with this metaphor for Jesus from the gospels, not least the story of Jesus and the Samaritan woman at the well (John 4:14), but this is a rarer reference to it in the Old Testament. Indeed the wording "For *with you* is the fountain of life" (my emphasis) makes this, for me, another Messianic verse, looking ahead to Christ. One of so many we are finding in the psalms.

The psalm ends (verses 10-12) with a plea for God's continued protection and blessing for His faithful.

The whole psalm is a reminder that, for David, God was not just to be called upon only when he needed help, like some "In emergency break the glass and pray" deity. David thought continuously on his relationship with the Lord, even in his "ordinary" or quieter days.

We too should keep God constantly in our minds, not just in our current times of stress but when the more normal times return too.

Sunday, 19 April 2020

Sunday, and a quieter day, with Sam and Ellen not working and a very good Sunday lunch – roast duck. Time also for cleaning, washing and ironing. It's funny how the weekly round of domestic chores has become something almost to look forward to, as a change from the otherwise sameness of much of the daily routine.

The brief colder and wetter snap has ended almost as soon as it began. I may have to run the sprinklers after all ...

Psalm 37:
The fates of the wicked and the faithful compared

Good morning. Today we have a slightly different psalm, indeed it reads almost more like a chapter of the Book of Proverbs, as it is not so much a prayer to God but a teaching for His people.

The psalmist tackles two timeless questions: why do godless people prosper, and when will God give His faithful their promised reward? These are both huge questions, and one psalm, even a long one, cannot fully explore the workings of God's purpose, but the psalmist invites us to hold onto three great truths:

Firstly, the prosperity of the wicked, for all it seems real at the time, is *transitory*.

Secondly, God *will* reward His faithful people, and their reward will be *everlasting*. It may be directly in that person's lifetime, it may be their children who are rewarded, or it may not be until our eternal life, but it is assured.

And thirdly, in the meantime, do not worry, do not fret, but trust the Lord.

"Do not worry, trust the Lord" – what a message for us in these difficult times.

Monday, 20 April 2020

Another day, another problem to solve, as Vicky's car has the "needs attention" light flashing on the dashboard. We find a garage that is open and take it down to them. Nothing wrong with the car – except a faulty warning light on the dashboard it seems! Ah well, it cost £40 (and quite a bit of worry) to find this out but could have been worse, I suppose.

In our "Senior Men's Bible Study Group" at our church, the consensus is that in this time of challenge and suffering, we should study the Book of Job. We have the first study today, and already I can see that this will be an interesting series, as the group is much more questioning, much more unsure than usual, and the range of opinions is much wider.

Today I also hear for the first time in nearly four weeks from a very close friend who has been desperately ill with the virus, both him and his wife. She is now fully better and he has also at last turned the corner. His tale will, we hope, now end well, but what a harrowing tale it sounds. "Not just the flu," he says, "most certainly not just the flu".

Psalm 38:
Sorrow for sin, and a plea for restoration

Good morning. Today's psalm is one of the best known of the Penitential psalms, where the psalmist, once again David, cries out to God as a sinner.

David starts by laying his woes before God (verses 1-8). He is suffering both mentally and, it seems, physically from the burden of his sin and his feeling of guilt. He feels separated from, cut off from God (verses 9-14), which compounds his miserableness.

Having described his agony, David confesses his sin (verses 15-20) and closes with a plea for rescue, to be reunited with God.

We do not know what particular episode in David's life led to this impassioned prayer, but it is impossible to miss the depth of his emotional stress here – not least because, unusually, he does not end the psalm in praise.

What I draw from the psalm is that when I sin, I need to turn not away from God in shame but *to* God for forgiveness – and the darker the sin, the deeper the need for God's healing and the more urgently I should lay it before Him.

Tuesday, 21 April 2020

The Queen's 94th birthday today, and surely one of the very strangest she can have had even in her very long life, with no public celebration, no appearance before the people.

Today our gardener re-appeared. He tells us that he has persuaded his insurance company that he is able to operate safely and with social distancing (fortunately he can get to our garden round the side of the house without needing to go through it), and he is raring to go. It is very good to see him, and while I was quite enjoying mowing the lawn (and not doing too bad a job, I think), I am delighted to hand it back to him both as one of the first small elements of normality beginning to return that we have seen since the lockdown started, and more prosaically because it is good that he can earn money again; we do want him to still be in business when the lockdown ends.

In the afternoon I add yet another string to my handyman bow as one of my shoes comes apart and needs mending. In the absence of being able to go to a cobbler it is wonderful what one can temporarily do with superglue!

Psalm 39:
The emptiness of life without God

Good morning. Like almost all the psalms we have met so far, today's is another written by David, and it appears to be from late in his life as he is looking back in reflection.

Although David is by now successful in worldly terms – king, wealthy, secure – the psalm shows him as fully aware of his frailty and impermanence before God. Apart from God, life is fleeting and empty, and David appeals for God's mercy to make his life more meaningful and bearable.

To me, the psalm shows David as uncharacteristically subdued: on the one hand, rather than extol God's greatness in public, as he so often does, he is silent in the company of non-believers (verses 1-2) for fear they will twist and misuse his words; and on the other, there is no ringing praise for the Lord at the end, as so often in his other psalms that we have looked at.

The honesty of the psalm also stands out: even someone as close to God as David can have self-doubts, can go as far as to pray verse 13: "Look away from me, that I may rejoice again". There are echoes here perhaps of Peter's feelings as Jesus looked at him in sorrow and love as he denied Him three times before the cock crew.

But even so, in the end David turns to God not away from Him; he still prays verses 7-8: "But now, Lord, what do I look for? My hope is in You, save me from all my transgressions", and verse 12a: "Hear my prayer, O Lord, listen to my cry for help; be not deaf to my weeping".

A psalm that leaves me with much to think about in my own relationship with God.

Wednesday, 22 April 2020

Another very small sign that life will eventually return closer to normality today, as our favourite fish and chip shop, Salt & Vinegar? (no, I don't know why the question mark is in their name either), returns to life – take-aways only of course, but, even so, great news. We order F&C all round and enjoy a feast. Together with the Wine Society, also now open again for deliveries, life is not all gloom …

Psalm 40: Waiting patiently for the Lord

Good morning. In today's psalm we once again see David, but in a rather different frame of mind from the subdued mood of the last couple of days. Here his patience in waiting for the Lord has been rewarded, and he is joyfully proclaiming his deliverance. Gone is the hesitation of yesterday's psalm, and once more he is emboldened to sing God's praises in the assembly, as in verse 9: "I proclaim righteousness in the great assembly; I do not seal my lips, as You know, O Lord".

The psalm also shows David's understanding of a great truth, that what God most of all wants from us is not ritual but our willing obedience. As the psalm says in verses 6-8: "Sacrifice and offering You did not desire ... burnt offerings and sin offerings You did not require. Then I said, 'Here I am, I have come ... I desire to do Your will, my God; Your law is within my heart'".

This resonates deeply for me with our current situation: it is not *bringing my body physically to church* that matters to God, valuable though it is for us to meet together and praise the Lord together, but *bringing my heart to God* that He most desires. And I can do that just as much in our current situation as before.

I also note with some amusement that although David starts the psalm as the very model of a patient servant – verse 1: "I waited patiently for the Lord" – he is soon back to urging the Lord to answer his prayer – verse 13: "Be pleased to save me, Lord; come quickly, Lord, to help me", and he closes with yet another plea for action: “You are my help and my deliverer; You are my God, do not delay”.

For the faithful, this desire for God to act, and act *now*, is so central that verse 13 is even incorporated in the Responses at our morning prayer: “O God, make speed to save us; O Lord, make haste to help us”. I never realised that every time we say these responses we are using the exact words originally written 3,000 years ago by King David!

Thursday, 23 April 2020

St George's Day. England could certainly do with the help of its patron saint to slay the dragon of disease!

A bit of fun today as a mug I ordered by mail order, with the words "Keep Calm – and play the trombone" on it, has arrived. And only two days after ordering it, too. Used immediately and much admired. Parts of the postal service seems to be working well, but other items take for ever to arrive – a parcel I sent our younger daughter a week ago has still not turned up (and it was sent first class).

In general, home deliveries seem to have got into their stride very well. What is noticeable is how much is delivered by people in ordinary private cars. One suspects that a lot of people whose main job has collapsed or who are on furlough have applied to be temporary delivery drivers. The actual delivery method has changed too with social distancing: they leave the parcel and ring the doorbell, and by the time one opens the door they are half way back down the drive. One shouts one's thanks as they retreat!

One thing home deliveries cannot do is haircuts! And after more than two months since I last visited a barber, I am in sore need of one. Vicky to the rescue with her sharp hair scissors, and a quite excellent job she does too. That feels much better!

Psalm 41:
A prayer when feeling sick or abandoned

Good morning. Once again we have another psalm of David, and in this psalm he is suffering twin evils: sickness and treacherous friends. David calls out to God for mercy and to be restored.

I find it very challenging when a Christian friend is ill, and my prayers for their recovery seem to have no effect. This psalm though forces me to think what our real sickness is, and what God's healing really entails.

In verse 3 David expresses his confidence that the Lord will restore the sick – or in some texts, sustain them. Reading the whole psalm through, one realises that this is not quite the same as a return to physical good health, much as we might pray for this for a friend or even for ourselves, but a promise of being restored to God's presence and favour.

In verse 4, David takes this further, as he understands that he is sick in his soul because of sin, and that it is this he needs God's healing for. The NIV text for the verse ends "heal me, for I have sinned against you" but other versions have "heal *my soul,* for I have sinned against you", which for me has the deeper resonance.

And so David is able to end the psalm by speaking not of earthly good health, but that God will, in the words of verse 12, "uphold me and set me in Your presence for ever".

Friday, 24 April 2020

A very sad day as we learn in the evening that Vicky's mother has died in her care home in Southport. Not of the virus, we are told, but of old age – she was suffering from extreme dementia, and for some time had been unable to communicate or even on some visits recognise Vicky. Vicky last visited her on 9 March; she had been going up to Lancashire every two to three weeks so the lack of an opportunity to say goodbye or even see her for the last seven weeks compounds the sense of loss. We wonder what funeral arrangements will be possible.

Before that it had been a Good Day, with the highlight being a delivery of bread flour. Shops have almost no bread flour for home baking, not because of a shortage of flour but because the mills have a shortage of 1 kg bags to put it in! Vicky scoured the internet and found a small mill in East Lothian that has flour by the 16 kg sack – so she bought one. It arrived very fast, in just two days, and we should be OK for a month at least.

Dinner was also a treat: Sam cooked us salmon en croûte. Quite delicious, and Ellen was visibly delighted to find what a good cook her boyfriend is! No doubt imagining many more such feasts …

Psalm 42:
Meditating on the need for God

Good morning. Today's psalm is the first in Book II of the Book of Psalms, and has both a different author from most of those we have studied so far and, for me, a different feel. It is marked as a psalm by the Sons of Korah, who, by the time this psalm was written, were assistants (possibly hereditary musicians) in the Temple.

The psalm is a deep meditation, a self-dialogue, about the psalmist's need for, indeed thirst for God. The opening verse, "As the deer pants for streams of water, so my soul pants for You, my God" is one of my favourite images – the psalmist has understood that while hunger is debilitating, thirst is far worse and works far more quickly to make life unbearable. To hunger for God is one thing, to thirst for God suggests altogether greater pain, greater urgency, greater need.

The psalmist alternates between introspective examination of his need and deep longing for God, and reminding himself that he should put his trust in God who will not abandon him. After listing his woes, the psalmist twice (verse 5 and verse 11) chides his own lack of faith and says "Why are you downcast, O my soul? … Put your hope in God".

I find the poetry in this psalm very powerful – there is much to enjoy in the imagery – but the verse I shall take away and think on most today is verse 6a: "My soul is downcast within me; therefore I will remember You". The word *therefore* is so powerful here: the implication for me is that when I am miserable, there is *all the more reason* to remember God.

Saturday, 25 April 2020

Vicky once again takes some shopping down to her father and, it being a Saturday, Sam goes with her. He seems in good health and fine form as they walk around his garden together, dutifully several metres apart. Otherwise, a quieter day; with everyone at home all the time the weekends lose a bit of their distinctiveness!

Vicky starts the planning for her mother's funeral with her brother, and I discover that her mother made me one of her two executors. As the other named executor died a few years ago I shall in theory be on my own. I think the two of us should be able to go up to Lancashire to attend the actual funeral, but it is not clear how many others will be able to attend and we certainly won't be holding a reception after it, alas.

Psalm 43: Putting our hope in God

Good morning. This psalm is in many ways a continuation of yesterday's – indeed, in some ancient manuscripts, the two are joined together in one psalm. They share the general theme of the psalmist debating with himself his response to depression and his need for God, and they culminate in the same conclusion, with the psalmist telling himself (verse 5) "Pull yourself together, trust God".

Having said that, for me there is a different feel to this psalm. It seems later in the psalmist's meditative process; more than half the psalm is upbeat, and there is less soul-searching and more emphasis on seeking the Lord. The heart of the psalm, verses 3 and 4, is a crescendo of approaching God and rising joy – the psalmist is brought first to the holy mountain, then to the Lord's House, then to the altar, then finally to God Himself. And the only possible response is delight and praise.

I think of the analogy of when I go to a test match. I set off for Lord's, I enter the ground, I take my seat in the stand, and then the players appear. The same sense of expectation, the same mounting excitement. Am I as excited at the thought of approaching God, I ask myself.

Sunday, 26 April 2020

Another quiet Sunday, another glorious day. The garden is bursting into life, and we sit out on the patio for lunch, enjoying another excellent barbecue.

The death toll from the virus has now exceeded 20,000, a level that the government said, right from the start, we would be "very lucky to avoid". Well, we haven't avoided it. But it is not clear how many of the 20,000+ are "lives cut markedly short", that is, young people losing perhaps decades of their expected lives, and how many are really "deaths brought slightly forward", that is, more senior people whose death has been accelerated but who were nearer the end of their natural span anyway.

But there are pieces of good news. The quite extraordinary creation of the Nightingale hospitals – 10 field hospitals built at breakneck speed around the UK (the London one in just eight days) has already provided 4,000 extra beds and will, when fully equipped and staffed, have over 16,000 beds. Even today, with just one quarter of their planned final capacity in operation, they are not full and have room for more patients, and despite dire warnings earlier on in the crisis the NHS has not so far threatened to run out of beds. Nor has it run out of ventilators, as companies as different as Dyson and Formula 1 racing teams have retooled their equipment to make ventilators for the NHS.

And finally, the daily death toll does seem to be easing. The trailing seven-day moving average peaked on 14 April, and has been lower every day now for over a week. Maybe with the Prime Minister back in No. 10 tomorrow, the government might start to consider easing some of the restrictions.

Psalm 44:
A plea for help from the battle-weary

Good morning. There is a familiar feel to today's psalm, which seems to run through so much of the life and experiences of God's people down the ages. And this is that, while we can see the mighty works God has done in the past, His hand is less visible to us in our generation. It seems it is ever thus.

Here the psalmists – again, the Sons of Korah – start by recalling and praising God's care and protection of their forefathers. This occupies the first eight verses of the psalm, and this opening section ends with the Hebrew word *Selah*, or "Pause". This is a word that often presages a change in sentiment in the psalm, and what a change we have here. Starting with verse 9, and continuing for the next 11 verses through to verse 19, the psalmists bemoan their current predicament. They are battle-weary and defeated, and feel that God has ignored them.

Often in the Old Testament this might be the cue for a prophet to lambast the people for straying from God's path, and urge them to return to the way of the faithful so that God will once again bless them. In this psalm, there is a rather different dynamic: the psalmists say "But we have not forgotten You, O God, nor have we abandoned Your ways, and even so our enemies are killing us" (verses 20-22), before renewing their plea to God for rescue (verses 23-26).

And yet even so, they do not base this prayer for deliverance on their own good works, but ground it firmly in God's grace; the psalm closes with the words "Rise up and help us; rescue us because of Your unfailing love". This is a surprisingly post-Reformation understanding of the nature of our relationship with God, based entirely on mercy and grace, and reminds me once again of the unchanging nature of God.

The whole psalm makes me want to sing that glorious hymn "O God, our help in ages past", and in particular the last verse, so apt for our current situation:

O God, our help in ages past,
Our hope for years to come,
Be thou our guide while troubles last,
And our eternal home.

Monday, 27 April 2020

The weather is definitely breaking – it is cooler today, and much rain is forecast for the next few weeks. It is almost as it the weather gods have got firmly in their minds "end of April = start of cricket season = rain", and have overlooked the complete absence of all organised sport at the moment. No cricket for at least another two months I suspect, alas.

Boris Johnson has returned to No. 10 today and resumed the reins of government. And his very first announcement is typically upbeat, and so totally different from the tone of the various ministers who have been standing in for him. He is far from everyone's cup of tea, but he exudes optimism and that in itself is valuable.

Psalm 45:
On the occasion of the king's wedding

Good morning. For a change today we have a song written for a king – thought possibly to be Solomon. It is to celebrate his wedding, and it is a beautiful song of praise and honour.

But even in Old Testament times it was also seen as much more than this, and was understood as referring not just to the earthly king but to the Messiah. From our vantage point of living after Christ's time on earth, this becomes even more clear, and the imagery of Christ as the King and the Church as His bride is one we are very familiar with.

As we read the Messianic psalms, I marvel afresh at how they were written 1,000 years before Christ yet so prophetically portray Him. So many prophesies, so many human authors down the centuries, yet so consistent in their message – it really is not possible to explain them except as God-inspired, ultimately God written.

Truly we are reading the Word of the Lord.

Tuesday, 28 April 2020

Much heavier and more persistent rain today, and noticeably cooler. The gardeners cannot come, unfortunately, because of the weather, and also our conservatory does indeed have a small leak, as we thought it might (see entry on 6 April). But Sam finds a conservatory man who is willing to come round, and he repairs the slippage in the roof pane – for a price! Not entirely convinced he isn't a cowboy (he looks very casual, no business card), but we will see how the pane holds up, and meanwhile the leaking has stopped for the moment.

Vicky continues to work away at the arrangements for her mother's funeral; we do now have the coroner's sign-off and the funeral has been set for Thursday week, 7 May at 2.00 pm. It will be in Southport and promises to be a very long day.

Psalm 46:
God our refuge and strength

Good morning. Today's psalm is a psalm of complete confidence in God. In the face of both natural disasters (verses 2 and 3) and war (verses 6-9), the psalmist declares that God will provide refuge, security and peace. His power is complete and His ultimate victory certain.

An unusual feature of the psalm is that, unlike many we have read, it does not start with a description of the psalmist's current distress, but launches straight into his statement of confidence in God's protection.

The psalm is also unusual in that in verse 10, it records God Himself speaking, as the text switches to the first person: "Be still, and know that I am God".

A psalm of enormous power and single-minded focus on the Lord.

Wednesday, 29 April 2020

The Prime Minister and his girlfriend announce the birth of a baby boy. Even the PM is not entirely sure whether it is his 5th, 6th or perhaps even 7th child of a somewhat chaotic personal life! We wish them well, but we also hope he is not too distracted: there was a palpable feeling of drift and indecision at the top of government while he was off sick. And he does need to get a grip on things: there is a growing sense of weariness with the lockdown, with more people out and about and much more traffic on the roads, and a definite exit plan with timings is becoming more urgently needed.

The preparations for the funeral continue; in the absence of the usual services and support from a church, it is going to be rather more of a DIY ceremony. Sam has been helping Vicky choose music on the internet, and I will be printing the order of service on my home PC. Fortunately, with only a very small family gathering the physical printing task is much reduced.

We learn on the Family Zoom call tonight that the parcel I sent to Royston on 16 April (first class, recorded delivery) has finally arrived. Much relief, but 13 days ... We also see for the first time their adorable new little kitten, a black and white cat who they have called Rosie-Monkey. Rosie for when she is being good (after Vicky's mother, whose middle name was Rosemary), and Monkey when bad! We end the day with an enormous take-away curry feast from Lal Akash. It is actually very good indeed, including a vindaloo for Sam (ordered in memory of his grandmother, whose favourite dish it was) – the first vindaloo he has ever tried, and he says it was "borderline too spicy, but extremely tasty". Brave man!

Psalm 47: God is the king of the whole earth

Good morning. We have another instance today where the psalm seems to me to follow on from the previous one, and indeed psalms 46-48 are often treated as a triplet, a three-part hymn of praise to the all-powerful sovereign God.

In Psalm 46 the psalmists focused on the security of God's people, noting how God had delivered them from one of their great enemies, and challenging the nations to observe that deliverance and stand in awe before God. In today's psalm, they say to those same people "Rejoice and be happy; the King of Israel is also the King of all the Earth, and so also your King".

For me there is a sense in this psalm of the psalmists struggling to find ways of expressing God's greatness, of describing it to the other nations. God is awesome beyond words, so the psalmists resort to describing what He has done instead. It reminds me of that great hymn "Immortal, invisible, God only wise", one of my favourites. The first verse is virtually a paraphrase of today's psalm:

Immortal, invisible, God only wise,
In light inaccessible hid from our eyes,
Most blessed, most glorious, the Ancient of Days,
Almighty, victorious, Thy great name we praise.

What a glorious hymn it is.

Thursday, 30 April 2020

A grey day, colder and much wetter than recently. The papers are full of "Captain Tom", a 99-year-old veteran who has captured the public's hearts by doing a sponsored walk around his garden to raise money for NHS charities. If it is not a pun in very poor taste, this "went viral", and once the newspapers got hold of the story the money flooded in in extraordinary amounts – eventually he raised over £30 million. Today is his 100th birthday and, as well as a card from the Queen (plus over 100,000 others!), he has been promoted to honorary colonel.

It shows that the public are hungry for good news stories; something our carping, criticising and negative media could do well to take note of (many might argue that the BBC are particularly at fault here, as at times they seem almost to adopt the stance of attacking everything the government does as their default position).

I write another newsletter for the Phoenix Masters, my livery past masters association. Although all events have been cancelled for the foreseeable future, there is quite a lot to write about, and the newsletter is one of my longer ones. I enjoy writing them, and it is good to stay in touch with the other members – and from the several replies I always get every time I issue one, the newsletters do seem to be appreciated.

Psalm 48: God's holy city is secure

Good morning. With today's psalm, we complete the triplet of psalms praising God our refuge, security and salvation.

Here the psalmists concentrate most on God's holy city, which is described as both beautiful and secure. There is a great air of permanence about the psalm, from verse 8b "God makes her secure for ever" to verse 14 "For this God is our God for ever and ever; He will be our guide even to the end". It suggests to me that the psalmists also had in mind the New Jerusalem, God's eternal city.

Today is the 1st of May, and as we confine April 2020 to the history books – not a month to remember with much enjoyment – I look for something to lighten the mood. And here in verse 5 we have an almost comic scene of Israel's enemies coming to Jerusalem: "they came, they marvelled, they fled". Shades of Caesar's *veni, vidi, vici*, only not quite as successful! But then Caesar was not up against the Lord ...

Friday, 1 May 2020

May Day, and I think we are all glad to see the end of April 2020. Not a month many people will remember with affection.

More IT problems first thing, as both Sam's and my emails are not working. It appears to be a fault at Microsoft, and it is a lot more serious for Sam who has a busy day "at the office" (also known as our dining room!) ahead of him. He manages to get through to his IT department, and together they solve it by the "frontal assault" approach – delete Outlook completely, clean all the links, reinstall a new version, and Go. And it worked, thank goodness.

Fortunately I have no such immediate pressures of deadlines, and by the time I come back from a walk to the shops for some top-up shopping, the various problems seem to have solved themselves. For the moment.

Moules marinière tonight, a real treat. We are in fact eating extremely well in the lockdown – restaurants may struggle to tempt us back to them!

Psalm 49:
The futility of relying on worldly possessions

Good morning. Our psalm today strikes a rather different tone; it is a psalm of instruction not praise, and for me seems more comparable to something from the book of Ecclesiastes.

The psalmist is keen to impress on his audience the importance of what he is about to say. The introduction (verses 1-4) is as long and as commanding as that of any medieval minstrel singing to a crowded hall – but his audience is not just a company of feasters but the whole world (verses 1 and 2), and it is not just a story or ballad he will give us but words of wisdom (verse 3), which quite literally mean life or death.

And his message is crystal clear: trusting in worldly possessions is futile. You cannot take them with you when you die and they cannot buy forgiveness for sins or eternal life.

Two verses in particular stand out for me, verses 7 and 15: "No man can redeem the life of another or give to God a ransom for him ... But God will redeem my life from the grave; He will surely take me to Himself".

Yet another instance where the Psalms point directly at Jesus, 1,000 years before His time on earth! We tend to think of teaching about eternal life as more a feature of the New Testament writers, but this psalm shows me that the psalmists were just as aware of the importance of the question, and had the same faith in God to give them everlasting salvation.

I am left reflecting again on the timelessness, the unchanging nature, of God.

Saturday, 2 May 2020

Saturday, and the fine weather returns for a day, though after a few greyer and wetter days the air is still quite cool. The daily rhythm of lockdown life continues, and Sam tries his hand at home baking. A magnificent wholemeal loaf is the result, kneaded by hand and baked in the oven – it is quite delicious with the trout we have for supper. There is much talk in the press of how a poor diet with lots of processed food can leave one more susceptible to the virus – not much risk of that here as, thanks to Vicky, most of our food is cooked from raw ingredients. We eat very well and healthily indeed! And interestingly, despite that, I am losing weight. Perhaps it is through not eating out – one suspects restaurant food is often very rich.

Psalm 50:
The judgment of God, the importance of faith

Good morning. Today we meet the psalmist Asaph for the first time. Asaph was one of David's chief musicians, and he is recorded as the writer of the second largest number of the psalms after David himself.

Asaph has a psalm of warning for us. He records the warning as spoken by God Himself, introduced in verse 1 as "The Mighty One, God, the Lord" – in the original Hebrew, "*El, Elohim, Yahweh*", the three main titles used for God in the Old Testament – to leave us in no doubt of the importance of the message. For God is about to judge the earth.

And to the surprise of God's people, He starts by turning to them. And what does He start with, and consider the most important thing in their relationship with God? It is the contrast between ritual and faith, between the outward show and the inner truth. God does not want sacrifices, but a true heart turning to Him in thanks, trust and praise.

This is exactly the message that Jesus himself gave on the Sermon on the Mount: "Not everyone who says to me 'Lord, Lord' will enter the Kingdom of Heaven, but only those who do the will of my Father".

Asaph thought this a message of the utmost importance. So did Jesus. Do I distinguish enough between ritual and true faith in my relationship with God?

Sunday, 3 May 2020

More home maintenance issues as one of the lights in the bathroom goes and, in trying to change it (never easy; it is a very fiddly fixture design), we break one of the retaining bits. Ah well, add it to the growing list of Things To Do When The Lockdown Ends.

Cooler today; we are back to more typical spring weather with warm days interspersed with cloudy and quite cool ones. In a way it is good that the sustained warm weather came early in the lockdown, when people's resolve to stick by the rules was at its highest. Fine weather now has the crowds out in large numbers.

Psalm 51:
A plea for forgiveness and mercy after great sin

Good morning. With today's psalm, we focus on a specific event in David's life: his adultery with Bathsheba and murder of her husband Uriah, and its aftermath. (The story is told in 2 Samuel 11-12.)

By the standards of the day, in which kings were all-powerful and could do what they liked, David had not done anything unusual. But he knew that by God's standards he had sinned, and had cut himself off from God by doing so.

Hence this powerful plea for mercy, forgiveness and cleansing. David confesses his sin to God and asks to be restored (verse 12) to a full relationship with Him.

Verses 16 and 17 show that David fully understands the learning we met in yesterday's psalm. "You do not delight in sacrifice, or I would bring it; you do not take pleasure in burnt offerings. The sacrifices of God are a broken spirit; a broken and contrite heart", he says, and here I picture David looking back on perhaps months of sacrifices after his adultery as he tried to erase his sin, and realising how ineffective they were without true contrition before God.

This is a tremendous psalm, pulsating with the agony of a sin-stricken soul that, even so, understands the wonder of the everlasting mercy of God.

Monday, 4 May 2020

Ellen's birthday today, and we celebrate with presents in the morning and a take-away pizza feast for dinner. I learn a new phrase from her – "Star Wars Day". What is that? May the fourth, of course, as in "May the Force (be with you)". A good day for her birthday!

Having spent all yesterday afternoon on a rather longer and more detailed "Laburnum essay" for my website, I am pleased to see it is well received by most of my circulation list. Most issues receive at least a few comments back, and they often lead to a good discussion. An excellent reason to keep doing them.

More encouraging news on the pandemic, with the lowest daily death rate yesterday since before the end of March, just 288. And London is coming out of the depth of it fast; it is no longer the worst affected area in the country (that is now the North West). So much so that the London Nightingale Hospital – all 4,000 beds of it – has been stood down as no longer needed. It really does seem that the lockdown and the Nightingale hospitals have saved the NHS from being over-run.

More good news too from the Continent of countries beginning tentatively to ease their own lockdowns. We were later going into ours and later to feel the full force of the virus, but hope is clearly growing in the public and the press that our restrictions will also start to ease before too much longer.

Psalm 52:
Leaving it to God to judge the wicked

Good morning. Today's psalm, like yesterday's, is rooted in a single historical event. Yesterday we saw David praying for forgiveness for his adultery with Bathsheba; today we see him praying in the aftermath of a mass slaughter of priests owing to the work of Doeg the Edomite. (The story is told in 1 Samuel 21 and 22:9-23.)

I find it remarkable that the psalms can in one place be dealing with matters of universal and eternal truth – such as Psalm 50 – and then, immediately following that, can delve right into specific events.

This psalm is notable for me in the way that David is not angrily railing at Doeg for his sins or demanding that God act to punish him. Rather, it is a contemplation of the evil Doeg has done, and a statement of confidence that God will judge the sinner without David's intervention. There is no doubt that David was angry, but he has not let his anger block his belief in God's ability to defeat evil.

After a pause for more contemplation (*Selah*), David continues with two responses: firstly, a general one, the reaction of the righteous (verses 6 and 7); and then his own reaction (verses 8 and 9). It is so easy to respond to great evil by asking God "Where are You when this sort of thing happens?", but David's response to a great evil was to reaffirm his faith in the Lord and His goodness.

This is the challenge today's psalm sets me.

Tuesday, 5 May 2020

A quiet day, as I complete the order of service for Vicky's mother's funeral in the morning (no way of going to our local printers, so all done and printed at home) and have a long video conference call in the afternoon. Two small ways in which life is very different from just two months ago.

But the gardeners come again, and also in the afternoon our window cleaner. Both of them can work without breaking the social distancing rules, and it is good to see them. Life is a long way from normal, but the links with The Before are not totally broken by any means.

Psalm 53:
All have sinned, all need God

Good morning. In today's psalm we have one of the minor puzzles of the Book of Psalms: it is almost exactly the same, word for word, as Psalm 14. Only in verse 5 does it differ.

We should not mind that we have a double measure of this psalm because in it, David is meditating on an important issue: why some people reject God, and what God will do in response.

We have I am sure all met the argument from non-believing friends: "There is no God, therefore I have not sinned against him, therefore I do not need him to rescue me from my sin". It is not an easy argument to confront or break down, especially when our friends live outwardly moral, law-abiding and successful lives.

But David says that, even so, they cannot escape the gaze of God; He sees everyone, and everyone is corrupt – even, in a bit of a sting in the tail for us, those who believe (verse 3: "there is no-one who does good, not even one").

I sense in this psalm a hint of frustration – verse 4: "Will the evildoers never learn?" – as David wonders why others cannot see what is so clear to him, why they remain so blind to God and their need for Him. And in his closing prayer, that God will restore His people, there is surely also the recognition that no-one can save themselves; only God can save us, only God can lead the ungodly to understand the error of their ways and to return to Him.

Wednesday, 6 May 2020

Time to mow the lawns again – although our gardeners were here yesterday, they were extremely busy keeping the weeding under control and, since I have a mower, I said I would do the lawns. Not a good idea: the alternate rain and hot sunshine of the last fortnight has produced a lot of growth, lots of new lush grass, and my little electric mower really struggled. It took nearly two hours to do the two lawns (on a good day it is under an hour for both) and produced seven bins' worth of grass cuttings, possibly the most ever.

But they do look much nicer once they are done. And I have earned my evening glass of wine!

Psalm 54:
If God is with me, who can stand against me?

Good morning. Once again we have a psalm of David, and it follows the pattern of many we have already seen: David is in trouble, and prays to God for rescue and for his enemies to be overcome. Then, part way through the psalm, his prayer turns into praise at the certainty that God will hear him and come to his aid.

Indeed I wonder myself if there is a double meaning in the praise at the end of the psalm (verses 6b and 7). In the NIV this reads "I will praise Your name, Lord, for it is good. For He has delivered me from all my troubles, and my eyes have looked in triumph on my foes".

On first reading, this reads straightforwardly as David saying "God has always rescued me in the past and has never abandoned me". But perhaps also there is the suggestion that the very act of prayer to God in his current difficulties has so reassured David that already he feels that he has overcome, that his current foes are defeated too.

As we learn from Romans (chapter 8 verse 31), "If God is for us, who can be against us". Or again, in Psalm 118 verse 6, "The Lord is with me; I will not be afraid. What can man do to me?".

One of the great messages of comfort in the Bible.

Thursday, 7 May 2020

A long day today as we went to Southport for Vicky's mother's funeral – a journey she has done many times over the years, but never for such a sad occasion, and today was almost certainly the last time. But the sun shone, the traffic was (understandably) amazingly light, the roads were clear and the service itself at the crematorium was actually very lovely and uplifting. And a rare chance to see our daughters in the flesh – the first time we had seen them since before the lockdown started over six weeks ago. We observed social distancing even so, but it was lovely to see them and chat, even if on a sad occasion.

The flowers in the wreath and sprays really were spectacular. They are usually taken to nearby hospitals and old people's homes, but that is not possible now so we took them home ourselves.

A very fast journey home, well under four hours for 245 miles; the M25 in particular was deserted, even at 6.00 pm, peak rush hour time usually. Vicky had made a casserole the day before, so dinner was on the table quickly too. It was delicious and a nice end to what was actually in a slightly strange way a very good day.

Psalm 55:
A prayer for help against treacherous friends

Good morning. Today we have another psalm of David, and once again he is beset by troubles. This time it appears to be the treachery of a close friend, who is spreading dissent and rebellion in the City of David and the Courts of the King.

For me the psalm shows "the four Fs" of David's response to the situation. He starts with Fear, and verses 1-5 give a very vivid description of David's mental state. He moves on to thinking of Flight (verses 6-8), a natural human reaction to difficulties, but neither practical for a king nor a solution that involves God.

Thirdly, we have David's Fury (verses 9-15), including in verse 15 the remarkably strong statement that David wishes, literally, that his enemies would go to Hell – though I note that, even here, David leaves the decision and the action to God.

Finally, David turns to Faith, his fourth F. In the last part of the psalm (verses 16 23), David turns to God for comfort and salvation.

This is a powerful psalm that I can really relate to – it is so full of human emotion, so much how we react to difficulties. And I focus on David's answer, summarised in verses 22 and 23b: "Cast your cares on the Lord and He will sustain you; He will never let the righteous fall ... As for me, I trust in You".

Friday, 8 May 2020

VE Day, and an unusual Friday bank holiday to mark 75 years since the end of World War II. Alas for the planned street-parties and celebrations, as we are all still kept largely indoors. And, as if to make matters worse, the weather is unusually glorious: so often the early May bank holiday is miserable and wet, but not this year! We mark it with a bottle of excellent Franciacorta, Italy's direct equivalent of Champagne and a very classy drink indeed (it can hold its own with France's finest), and Sam and Ellen cook a "flamiche", a leek and cheese flan from his new baking book, for supper. It is quite delicious.

The Queen speaks to the nation again – after doing so just four times in her reign before this year (other than her Christmas messages) she has now addressed us twice in a month. And it reminds us that outside our self created little bubble, as we have been concentrating on Vicky's mother's funeral, the news of the progress of the disease, which a week ago had looked more hopeful, has turned more gloomy again, with death rates returning to higher levels. The UK's death rates are now among the worst in Europe per million of population – although with the caveat that every country is measuring the numbers in different ways. No-one is really sure why, but it is enough for the government to predict a very slow exit from the lockdown.

Psalm 56:
Trust in God, praise for His Word

Good morning. For the last few days we have been in a run of psalms where David is crying out to the Lord for help in a time of trouble, and today's is another which follows the pattern of plea for rescue, confidence that God will come to his aid, followed by praise for salvation.

One might wonder why the Book of Psalms contains so many individual psalms that are so similar. There are over 70 psalms attributed to David and in the great majority he is calling on the Lord from a position of danger. But each of them is slightly different and shows a different facet of David's faith.

Today's is striking for the repeated use of the phrase "In God, whose word I praise, in God I trust". It appears in verse 4 and twice in verses 10-11. Why does David trust God? Because he knows Him. How does he know Him? Through His Word.

Trusting in God is a central theme in this psalm, and David's trust is based not only on his experience of the Lord in action – he has been rescued from his enemies many times before – but also on diligent study of God's Word in the Scriptures.

And with that trust, David can boldly declare (verse 4b and again verse 11b) "I will not be afraid. What can man do to me?"

Saturday, 9 May 2020

A day of domestic chores, as we hoover and clean the floors, do the washing and ironing, and I wash my car. The long run to Southport and back on Thursday not only showed how generally grubby it was, but also resulted in far more dead insects on the windscreen than usual. We wonder why this might be – perhaps the air is cleaner with less traffic, allowing more insects to breed, or perhaps there are simply fewer cars on the roads for them to impale themselves on!

Sam turns again to his baking book and produces some wonderful cheesy bacon rolls – rolls with bacon and cheese chopped into them at the baking stage. Extremely scrumptious, but if he goes on baking like this our waistlines will explode!

My uncle Charles rings me with a typically unusual request. He was quite ill with the virus for nearly two weeks and, although fit, he is well over 70, so it is good to hear he is back to his usual irrepressible self!

Psalm 57:
Taking refuge under God's wings

Good morning. Today we once again see David calling on the Lord for help in times of trouble. The heading to this psalm says that David was hiding in a cave at the time, after fleeing Saul (the story is in 1 Samuel 22-24).

Two things stand out for me in this psalm. The first is the contrast between the temporary physical safety that David has found in the cave, and the permanent spiritual security and salvation that he knows he will only find with God. Even while temporarily safe, hidden from his enemies, he calls out to God for the greater security of God's mercy.

There is a familiar picture in verse 1b of God providing shelter and safety as a mother hen shields her chicks from danger. One recalls that Jesus quoted the same image when looking over Jerusalem: "Jerusalem, Jerusalem ... how often I have longed to gather your children together, as a hen gathers her chicks under her wings" (Matthew 23:37).

And the second thing that stands out for me is the way in which the very act of prayer reassures David. As the psalm progresses, the tone becomes less fearful and more confident; less a plea for help and more a song of praise. I sense that when, in verse 5, David prays the psalm's main prayer for the first time: "Be exalted, O God, above the heavens; let Your glory be over all the earth", it is mainly in hope, but then he recovers his confidence (verse 7: "My heart is steadfast, O God, my heart is steadfast"), and the second time he prays the prayer, in verse 11, it is with full assurance that God *will* be exalted above the heavens.

Non-Christian friends sometimes ask me what the point of praying to an all knowing God is: "Surely he knows what you need or want before you ask?" This psalm gives an answer: the prayer is for the benefit not of God, but the person praying. It is David who feels better, more secure, closer to God after praying this psalm.

Sunday, 10 May 2020

A quiet Sunday, though we are maintaining the tradition of proper Sunday lunches to differentiate Sundays from other days, and enjoy one of Vicky's finest roasts – rib of beef, which I honour with the inaugural use of a smart new tablecloth and some recently unearthed fine glasses.

The weather starts warm and sunny, but a cold front comes and by evening we are closing windows and reaching for our jerseys. The colder weather has not yet finally left us, for all that it is May.

This evening the Prime Minister has spoken to the nation on the next stages of the national strategy to defeat the virus. He is cautiously optimistic, and announces a few limited relaxations, but for a man who has made a career out of colourful language, elaborate metaphor and arresting imagery, it is a very different style of address from others he has made, laden with caution and caveats. The relaxations are minor and limited, the timescale for the further re-opening of society extended, and the warnings that there will be no hesitation in putting the brakes back on if matters deteriorate again are repeated and insistent. He comes across as very different from the ebullient optimist he was when he became PM.

And news from the Continent suggests he is right to be cautious, as we hear that in Germany, which has so far escaped the virus with fewer deaths than most European countries and has already begun to relax their lockdown, is now seeing a resurgence in infection rates. It is fair to say that more governments than just the one in Berlin will be watching their situation extremely closely in the next few weeks.

Psalm 58:
Calling on God to judge the world's rulers

Good morning. Today we have another of the Imprecatory psalms, a form of psalm we first met in Psalm 35. Here the psalmist, again David, is considering the rulers and judges of the day and accusing them of false judgments, of not pursuing true justice. He calls on God to act against them, to judge the judges, and to destroy them.

The psalm closes with a picture of the righteous rejoicing at the downfall of their wicked overlords. The imagery is graphic and even savage, as (verse 10) they "bathe their feet in the blood of the wicked", and (verse 11) they acclaim the God who has inflicted this punishment on them.

This is a harsh and somewhat grim psalm, as indeed the Imprecatory psalms often are; there is little sign of tolerance or mercy, and unusually an almost complete absence of praise at the conclusion. I sense that David was feeling very bitter, possibly towards Saul and those judges who curried favour with him by passing judgment on David when he was a fugitive, in effect condemning him to death if he was caught.

But even in the depths of his bitterness, David remembers to call out to the Lord, to entrust the matter to Him, to rely on God's perfect judgment. That is the message I will take away from this psalm this morning.

Monday, 11 May 2020

A tense day on the IT front as I tackle a long-standing problem with our emails. The technology they rely on is increasingly outdated and fragile, and after one too many minor crises and data losses I bite the bullet and change to a more modern and robust platform. A major operation that takes all morning, but all goes well, in fact surprisingly smoothly, and we are up and running again by mid-afternoon. I breathe a huge sigh of relief. But the new system is slightly less convenient and rather more expensive – why is IT always like this?!

In the evening Vicky and I make use of the slight relaxations in the lockdown and walk to a couple of friends for a chat. We stand on the pavement, and they in their front garden the required two metres from us, but it is very good to see them in the flesh – phone calls and video conferencing cannot replace that, however good they are. It is however cold, much colder than at the weekend with a nasty wind, so we do not prolong the visit!

Psalm 59:
The strength of God, the power of faith

Good morning. We are once again with David in today's psalm, as he again faces treacherous enemies and cries out to the Lord for help and protection. It is striking how many enemies David had, both before he became king and even once he had ascended the throne, and we might think it odd that a man so close to God, Israel's greatest human king, should have been so beset. Perhaps the idea is less strange when we reflect on Jesus, the Son of David and Israel's heavenly King, and how many more enemies He had. Evil will always oppose Good, and try to eradicate it.

David alternates in this psalm between describing his predicament and declaring his strong confidence in God. At the end of describing his attackers (verses 3-8), he declares his faith in verses 9-10a: "You are my strength, I watch for You; You, O God, are my fortress, my God on whom I can rely". But instead of finishing the psalm there, he returns to considering his attackers again and their fate, before once more returning to his faith in God with the slightly different refrain (verse 17) "You are my strength, I sing praise to You; You, O God, are my fortress, my God on whom I can rely".

This psalm is a great example of the Hebrew writing style of "emphasis by repetition". The repetition is both of individual words and whole sections; the repetition gives emphasis to David's prayer, and the subtle changes in the individual words used gives a depth and intensity to his feelings. For example, in verse 5 David calls on God as "O Lord, God Almighty, God of Israel" (in Hebrew *"Yahweh, Elohim Tzevaot, Elohi Israel"* or "Covenant God, God of Hosts, God of the chosen people") – David is calling on God in every way he knows, so great is his need for His help and protection. And in the refrains (verses 9 and 17), we see how, just by praying the prayer, David's mood is changing, from "watching for God" in the first refrain to "praising God" by the end of the psalm.

For me, this psalm resonates with strength and power: the strength of God, and the power of David's faith in Him.

Tuesday, 12 May 2020

A quieter day at home, and I take the opportunity to make progress on a book I am writing. It has been "on the go", on and off, for about 10 years, but the lockdown has enabled me to get it to the stage where I can at last start talking to a potential publisher. He is cautious, but will consider it and come back to me with a publication proposal and costings.

The Prime Minister's statement on Sunday evening appears to have caused some confusion. It wasn't the clearest of statements – I don't think it could have been given the very tentative nature of easing a lockdown, with so many more uncertainties than when the country was slammed shut – but there is now genuine uncertainty about who can or should go to work, not to mention how they will get there. Outside London most people drive or walk to work, but in London public transport dominates, and social distancing is just not possible on the tube, even outside rush hour. A real problem.

Psalm 60:
Trust in the Lord in times of strife

Good morning. Today we have a psalm from the heat of battle. David has by now become king, and is leading Israel on a multi-front war, which appears for the moment not to be going well. He cries out to God in three ways:

A cry for mercy and restoration (verses 1-3): David sees the reverses on the battlefield as a sign of God's displeasure and asks for His mercy and that His salvation be restored to His people.

A statement of hope and trust (verses 4-5): Although David felt that God Himself had caused Israel's defeats, he does not hesitate to continue to unfurl his banner of allegiance to the Lord. His trust in God is not broken by God's deserved disciplining.

A confident prediction of ultimate victory (verses 6-8): David here acts as a prophet, relaying God's words of assurance that he will be victorious and lead Israel to triumph.

The psalm ends (verses 9-12) with David fully reassured and restating his complete trust in God. "The help of man is worthless", David declares, "with God we shall gain the victory".

The power of this psalm is David's ability to bring his problems to God and leave everything in His hands. God will not ignore us or abandon us if we trust in Him.

Wednesday, 13 May 2020

The gardeners come again and put in a major stint this morning – like my hair, the garden has been getting rather unkempt and they spend all morning pruning and weeding. The front garden in particular has a lot to clear away; it is very much a spring garden, at its best in April and early May, but by now there is a lot to clear. They do a good job and it is all set for the roses, which start coming at this time of year.

Before the roses, the last thing to flower in the front garden is usually our laburnum tree. We were surprised when we moved to the house that a house named Laburnum did not have a laburnum tree, and we planted one for the millennium in 2000. It flowered beautifully every year – it is a lovely tree, one of my favourites – but it died in 2018. We planted another that autumn and held our breath to see if it would flourish: in 2019 it did not flower at all, as it was perhaps too young, but this year it is flowering bravely and a wonderful sight to see. We are delighted and look forward to it growing big and strong over the coming years.

Psalm 61:
An urgent cry for help

Good morning. There is an air of desperation, even of exhaustion, about today's psalm, another psalm of David, and it is clearly a prayer of great intensity and urgency. The opening verse sets the tone: "Hear my cry, O God; listen to my prayer" – David knew that God always hears our prayers, but it seems that he was in particular need at this time, and urgently wanted God not just to passively hear his prayer, but actively listen to it, attend to it, answer it.

This desire for a response sets David's prayer very much apart from the prayers of ritual, the liturgies and set prayers that are said as part of communal worship. It makes me reflect on the difference between praying with one's lips and praying with one's heart, a distinction that David knew well.

David continues in the same desperate vein; he is praying (verse 2) "from the ends of the earth" – which might be literally, if he was in some far part of his kingdom, or perhaps figuratively, as in at the end of his tether – and his "heart grows faint". That is the modern wording, but the King James Bible has the more heartfelt "From the end of the earth will I cry unto thee, when my heart is overwhelmed". And, in verse 4, he says "I long to dwell in Your tent". Again, we hear the urgency.

But despite his desperation, David maintains his faith and trust in the Lord and ends, as so often, in praise: "Then I will ever sing in praise of Your name and fulfil my vows day after day".

There is deep emotion in this psalm.

Thursday, 14 May 2020

Another day of home maintenance as we try to sort out our fridge. The thermostat is we think faulty, and while it is mostly keeping things cool, the inside is icing up alarmingly and there is a big block of ice at the back, which is growing. We defrost it and remove it; it weighs more than 3 kg! A new fridge looms: another thing to address when we are able to get to the shops.

More signs of life tentatively restarting as golf clubs, among other sporting venues, are allowed to re-open. But there is great confusion still about who, and how many people, one is allowed to go and visit while still observing social distancing. And London's public transport challenges remain unresolved. We are a long way still from a permanent solution to the virus crisis.

Psalm 62:
The peace of the Lord

Good morning. Today's psalm, another attributed to David, is unusual in that it is neither a prayer nor a song of praise. It is more of a quiet meditation.

David seems to be facing challenges again, possibly the rebellion of Absalom (described in 2 Samuel 15-18), but, unlike in many of his psalms, he neither starts by describing his predicament nor asks God for assistance. Indeed, in the whole psalm there is not one word of fear or despair – nor, even more unusually, a word of direct praise. Instead, the psalm is a reflection on David's need for God, on the fact that true salvation and peace of mind can come only from God.

What a strong word "Peace" is. For most of us, most of the time, it is a "nice to have" but no more; only those who do not have peace, either in their outward lives or in their inner thoughts, can really value it and know how much we need it. Jesus certainly knew the value of peace when He said to His disciples (John 14:27) "Peace I leave with you; my peace I give you … Do not let your hearts be troubled and do not be afraid". Unlike worldly peace, which is usually defined as merely the absence of conflict, only God's peace offers complete assurance, the absence of fear for either the present or the future.

This is what David understood, and what underpins this psalm of meditation. Verse 1 declares "My soul finds rest in God alone", and the uniqueness of God's peace is a theme throughout the psalm – verse 2: "He alone is my rock";

verse 5: "Find rest, O my soul, in God alone"; verse 6: "He alone is my rock and salvation".

Trust in the Lord, and He will give you His peace.

Friday, 15 May 2020

The end of the first week after the Prime Minister's statement on (slightly) easing the lockdown, and life is noticeably busier. More people about, more passengers on the buses, and considerably more cars on the roads near us. The daily death tolls do continue though; they are at a lower level (and new infections are at a much lower level, especially in London), but the virus has not left us and the next few weeks will show if we have relaxed the lockdown too soon. Anxious times for the authorities ...

We leave such weighty matters to others as we have a celebration tonight: Sam has secured a full grade promotion at work and we are opening the bubbly. It is his second full grade move up in just 18 months and, from watching and listening to the effort he puts in each day as he works from our dining room, I am sure it is well deserved.

Psalm 63: The desire for God's love

Good morning. Today's psalm is another psalm of David, and is thought to come from the same period of his life as yesterday's, when he was alone and hiding from many enemies. In Psalm 62, David was meditating on the true peace that comes only from God; in this psalm, he expands on that thought and declares that the love of God is the thing he desires most of all.

There are two dominant themes in the psalm: the earnestness and urgency of David's longing for God (verse 1: "my soul thirsts for You, my body longs for You, in a dry and weary land where there is no water"), and the complete satisfaction he finds in God's love (verse 3: "Your love is better than life", and verse 5: "my soul will be satisfied as with the richest of foods").

Even "through the watches of the night" (verse 6) David meditates on the Lord. Only the sleepless see all the watches of the night, and I have here a vivid picture of David, unable to sleep because of his worries, but even so turning his thoughts not to his earthly predicament but to God.

This is a psalm of single-minded concentration on God and His love. It challenges me to think about what is really important in life.

Saturday, 16 May 2020

Sam and Ellen make use of the relaxations in the lockdown to drive to the Surrey Hills and go for a long walk. They take a picnic and are away for about six hours – it is probably longer than all the amount of time Ellen has been out of the house put together since she came to stay with us! The pattern is repeated across the country as the weekend and the better weather encourage people out of their homes, and Sam reports a much increased amount of traffic on the A3, though once in the Surrey Hills they had little difficulty finding somewhere to walk alone.

In the evening we have a wine tasting with our elder daughter and her housemate. She opens exactly the same bottle as we do (a very fine white Burgundy from the Côte Chalonnaise) and we compare notes by Zoom. The wine is delicious and the joint tasting great fun – this is one use of the video call technology we have all so rapidly mastered that might survive the end of the lockdown!

Psalm 64:
Nothing is hidden from God

Good morning. We have a fascinating psalm today that has multiple layers. It is another psalm of David and, as so often, it starts with a prayer for deliverance from his troubles (verses 1-6) before he expresses his confidence in God's response and judgment on the wicked (verses 7-10).

David's problems in this psalm concern conspiracies against him. Men are plotting behind his back, spreading slander, exciting the crowds against him – verse 3: "They sharpen their tongues like swords and aim their words like deadly arrows". This is one of David's favourite word-images; we have seen it several times in recent psalms, for example in Psalm 52 verse 2, Psalm 57 verse 4 and Psalm 59 verse 7. David certainly did not believe that "Sticks and stones may break my bones, but words will never hurt me"!

But just as the conspirators plot in secret and (verse 4) hope to strike suddenly, so equally suddenly (verse 7) the tables are turned. God the All-seeing has seen their plots and strikes them down. Ruin is brought onto those plotting David's ruin, and their words are turned back on them (verse 8).

For me, the whole psalm is messianic. David's prayer to God about his predicament looks forward to the conspiracies against Jesus in His last week in Jerusalem – verses 5 and 6, "They encourage each other in evil plans, they talk about hiding their snares; they say, 'Who will see it?' They plot injustice and say, 'We have devised a perfect plan!'", describe the actions of Caiaphas and the other leaders completely. And God's response in verse 8: "He will turn their own tongues against them and bring them to ruin; all who see them will shake their heads in scorn" was vividly played out in the fate of Judas Iscariot.

There are no secrets from God, nothing is hidden from Him.

Sunday, 17 May 2020

With the garden centres now open again we have decided to set up some tomato and cucumber plants in the greenhouse. This requires clearing out the greenhouse and getting it ready, and revamping the watering system, and the gardeners have agreed to fit this in on their next visit. And so in time-honoured style I spend much of the afternoon today getting the greenhouse ready for the gardeners to tidy – by the time I finish I have done two-thirds of the work myself!

Psalm 65:
God the abundant Provider

Good morning. Today we have a psalm that is a glorious hymn of praise to our provider-God. God's blessings are recalled, and He is praised for His abundant provision for our needs.

The psalm is in three stanzas. In the first (verses 1-4), God is praised for His forgiveness. And having forgiven us, God welcomes His people into His presence (verse 4: "Blessed are those You choose and bring near to live in Your courts"). This is a full restoration and redemption, not a grudging acceptance or toleration of our misdeeds.

In the second (verses 5-8), the psalmist acknowledges God as the all-powerful Creator God. God is praised as the Creator of the whole world, not just Israel: in verse 5 He is described as "the hope of all the ends of the earth and of the farthest seas", in verse 7 He is portrayed as stilling "the turmoil of the nations", and in verse 8 the psalmist declares "Those living far away fear Your wonders".

Finally, the third stanza (verses 9-13) is a wonderful hymn of praise for a bountiful harvest. God's people are blessed with a cornucopia of good things, their carts overflow (verse 11), even the desert is productive (verse 12), so much so that the very land shouts for joy (verse 13).

For me, the overwhelming message of this lovely psalm is that God goes far beyond what we deserve, gives us far more than we need. He does not just forgive our sins, but restores us to His presence completely. He is not just the Creator of

Israel, but of the whole world. He does not just feed us, but showers us with abundance. What a wonderful provider-God we have.

Monday, 18 May 2020

Vicky tries the garden centre for tomato grow-bags but there is a long queue (they are only allowing a few people into the shop at a time) so she comes home empty-handed. Sam decides that when he goes back to the office, rather than commute on the crowded trains, he will bicycle, and starts to get his bike in order – it has a puncture, though, which proves elusive and may need a new inner tube completely.

Meanwhile, for the second day running, the daily death toll is well under 200, the lowest since the lockdown started. And Monday morning traffic on the road outside our house is almost up to normal levels. Life is slowly returning – but the economic news of closed businesses and financial losses is alarming.

Psalm 66:
Thanking God for answered prayer

Good morning. Our psalm today is a general psalm of thanksgiving, and is the first psalm for over two weeks that is not attributed to David. It is a psalm where the psalmist moves from the universal to the communal to the personal, concentrating his thanks at each step.

The psalmist starts with a call to "all the earth" (verse 1) to acclaim God for His power and sovereignty, and calls on the whole world to bow down to the Lord, to sing praises to His name (verse 4), to marvel at His awesome works (verses 5-8). He then focuses on what God has done for His people (verses 8-12), testing them, refining them, preserving them. Finally in this trilogy the psalmist turns to himself – the text switches to the first person singular for the rest of psalm – and he thanks God for his own salvation (verses 13-20), and especially for answers to prayers.

I note in particular verses 13-15, where the psalmist has clearly made certain promises to God (no doubt along the lines of "If you rescue me from this danger then I will …"), and now is fulfilling them gladly with the best of sacrifices. How easy it is to promise things to God when we need His help, and then "forget" once we are safe again, or honour our promises in the meanest and cheapest way we can. The psalmist knows that this is not what God wants!

A great psalm of public and private gratefulness for mercies received, a great example of giving thanks.

Tuesday, 19 May 2020

We continue to prepare the greenhouse for growing vegetables and the gardeners and I complete a project I have long wanted to do – putting in a better irrigation and water system with a multiple tap for the various hoses we run. It works very well, and exactly as I had planned. Another thing that has taken the enforced staying at home of the lockdown for me to get round to doing.

Alas, part two of setting the greenhouse up – buying grow-bags and tomato plants – is less successful. Despite getting to the garden centre early, there is already a long queue and we leave empty-handed. They are being extremely carefully at how many people they let in to the centre – 28 people maximum at any one time (in a 4,400 m2 area, most of which is outdoors!) – but they say this is simply government advice. The irony is that in the shop each person may have over 100 m2 of space for social distancing, but in the queue to get in we have about 6 m2 each! Not for the first time, the rules on relaxing the lockdown seem to be made up on the spot and lacking in clarity, consistency and common sense.

Psalm 67:
A call for God's blessing

Good morning. We have a beautiful psalm this morning, a call for God's blessing on His people and a prayer also for the spread of God's Word.

The psalm starts by echoing what is known as Aaron's blessing, a blessing that God instructed Moses and the leaders of the Israelites to use for the people: "The Lord bless you and keep you; the Lord make His face shine on you and be gracious to you; the Lord turn His face toward you and give you peace" (Numbers 6:24-26). This beautiful blessing was usually used by the Jews as a dismissal at the end of a liturgy – we sometimes still use it today ourselves in the same way – but here it opens the psalm, and sets the tone for the prayer that follows.

The rest of the psalm is strongly prophetic of the Great Commission, as the psalmist prays for God to be known throughout the world, and for "all the peoples" to praise God, for "the nations of the earth" to be glad and sing for joy at His rule (verses 3-5). It is remarkable that the psalmist was writing this so many centuries before Christ instructed His disciples to spread the news of God to all the world.

Having opened with a prayer requesting God's blessing, the psalmist closes more definitively with the straightforward statement "God will bless us" (verse 7a). What a wonderful thing that, because of the Great Commission and the spread of God's Word, we too can join the psalmist in saying this with the confidence of true belief.

Wednesday, 20 May 2020

At our third attempt we are successful at the garden centre! By arriving over half an hour before it opens we are number two in the queue, and once it does open we are in and out quite quickly. And 100% successfully too, with grow-bags aplenty and tomatoes, cucumbers, beans and beetroot plants. But the lack of thought about how to space people out is shown even more starkly, because when the 28 people they are allowed to let in enter … we all make a beeline for the vegetable section and stand pretty much on top of each other! It seems the UK is becoming a nation of grow-your-own vegetable growers as well as bake-at-home breadmakers.

More signs of life in the High Street: the building plot near us, which has been silent for eight weeks, has people working on it again; our Chinese take-away (see entry for 25 March) is open again; and there is a queue at the bank when I go to pay in a cheque. The empty streets and silent shops are slowly reawakening.

Psalm 68:
God's power, protection and provision

Good morning. After a run of shorter psalms we have a much meatier one today, and one that many commentators consider quite challenging to understand. Perhaps that is because the subject matter of the psalm, God's awesome power, is itself difficult for us to comprehend.

The psalm is a litany recalling three aspects of God and His care for His people: His Power, which is absolute; His Protection of Israel, which is complete and assured; and His Provision for them, which covers both their temporal and spiritual needs. The complexity of the psalm comes from the psalmist mixing recollections of historical blessings and expressions of confidence of future grace, the whole producing an overwhelming sense of God's sovereignty and the psalmist's desire to praise Him.

For me, this is a psalm to read and be engulfed in, not one to pick out this verse or that phrase. But I do highlight especially verses 19-20, where the psalmist pauses for breath half way through the psalm and summarises where we have got to so far: "Praise be to the Lord, to God our Saviour, who daily bears our burdens. Our God is a God who saves; from the Sovereign Lord comes escape from death".

Read and enjoy the psalmist's sense of awe at our God.

Thursday, 21 May 2020

The hottest day of the year so far, and we had just decided it was too hot for gardening when about two dozen border plants turn up at the door. I had ordered them online three weeks ago when the garden centres were closed and growers were despairing of selling their stock, as a way of helping them in their predicament, and finally they arrive. The selection is fairly random, and the timing could not really be worse – not only on a really hot day, but also arriving just as the garden centres are back open again! But hopefully it helped out a grower, and we turn to and plant all 24 of them in the heat. And I then use our new irrigation system to give the whole garden a good soaking.

The news seems to have settled into a quieter rhythm. The general trend is for continued but slow improvement in the health picture (in infection rates, hospital utilisation levels, numbers of deaths) but continuing attrition on the economic front, the latest sign of which is an auction of gilts with negative yields. On the health front, this will be a long haul, with no cathartic "We are free" moment, no single declaration of victory and return to normality. And on the economic front, it promises to be an even longer one.

Psalm 69: A call for rescue from deep waters

Good morning. For the second day running we have a substantial psalm to enjoy; indeed today's psalm is one of the longest of David's prayers to the Lord when in difficulties, and the depth of his despair is seldom more intense than here. He is overwhelmed with grief and fear and pours out all his agonies to God in a long and heartfelt prayer for help.

The psalm follows a familiar pattern, as David first describes his distress and the attacks he is enduring (verses 1-21), then calls on God to exercise His judgment against his oppressors (verses 22-28), before finally ending with praise and the assurance that God would save His people. I marvel that even when David is close to losing hope (verse 2b: "I have come into the deep waters; the floods engulf me"), even when his prayers are seemingly ignored (verse 3: "I am worn out calling for help; my throat is parched. My eyes fail, looking for my God"), he still calls on the Lord, still has the confidence to pray for rescue.

The psalm has also traditionally been seen as messianic, foretelling the enemies Jesus would face (verse 4: "Those who hate me without reason outnumber the hairs of my head; many are my enemies without cause, those who seek to destroy me"), and predicting the treatment He would receive at their hands. Verses 22 28 then read as a prophecy of the fate of the whole Jewish nation, and the close, verses 35-36, as looking forward to the New Jerusalem.

David's life was a lesson in never giving up, never abandoning belief and trust in God, and this psalm is for me the epitome of constancy of faith.

Friday, 22 May 2020

A much cooler day, and we make use of it to complete setting up the vegetables in the greenhouse. The new irrigation system works well, and it is good to have the tomatoes and cucumbers all set.

A good friend comes round for coffee – lockdown style. We are now allowed to meet singly and out of doors, and he bicycles to us to sit with me on our front lawn, dutifully two metres from me. He comments that the traffic is growing noticeably heavier, with even some traffic jams on the main roads. It is certainly noisier in our front garden than earlier in the month! But still very good to see him.

The news is dominated by arguments over when, and how, to allow the travel and tourism industry to restart. No-one doubts the importance of holidays as a sign of normal life restarting and something for people to look forward to, but I can't help feeling that there are more serious economic issues to resolve.

Psalm 70: An urgent plea for help

Good morning. After the longer psalms of the last two days we have a much shorter one today. It is one we have in fact seen before: it is an excerpt of Psalm 40, as the psalmist, again David, repeats with only slight modifications verses 13 17 of his earlier psalm.

The psalm is an urgent plea for help. David is in mortal danger (verse 2: "May those who seek my life ...") and needs immediate rescuing (verse 1: "Hasten, O God, to save me; O Lord, come quickly to help me"). So strong is the sense of urgency that the psalm also closes with it (verse 5b: "O Lord, do not delay").

I see this small psalm as a prayer "for use in dire emergencies". David was certainly happy to pray at length to the Lord when he had the time; many of his psalms are meditative, reflective and extensive. But, equally, there were times when he just wanted to shout "Help! I need help *now*!", and this psalm seems to me to be one for use in such desperate circumstances.

Yet even so, David finds room for praise as well (verse 4: "May all who seek You rejoice and be glad in You; may those who love Your salvation always say, 'Let God be exalted'").

And finally, in closing his prayer, David recognises that the Lord is his only hope (verse 5a: "You are my help and my deliverer"); he relies wholly on the Lord, and trusts that He would answer this complete faith.

Saturday, 23 May 2020

With Sam and Ellen out almost all day visiting Ellen's mother in the West Country – day trips and brief visits to one other person are now allowed – we have a quieter day at home, with weather more like April than late May: hot sun, then clouds, then rain, then high winds and ending quite cool!

Another sign of life returning a bit more to normal is that other news is beginning to make itself heard above the blanket coverage of disease, death rates and depressing economics. The newspapers have almost totally ignored the outside world for two months, but international politics is continuing, and China is using the fact that the West is still very much pre-occupied with the virus to tighten its grip on Hong Kong, with a new security law that in effect ends Hong Kong's limited freedoms. Much condemnation from the international community, but China will ignore it: one consequence of the animosity towards China for their part in spreading the virus is that they no longer even pretend to care about world opinion. To quote the chant made famous by Millwall fans in the 1980s, "Nobody likes us, we don't care; we're big and strong, oppose us if you dare". This new belligerent attitude from China is not a good sign for the world.

Psalm 71:
A strong faith in old age

Good morning. In today's psalm our anonymous psalmist is towards the end of his life, reflecting on a long association with God and seeking God's continued protection in his old age.

The psalmist opens with a general prayer for God's assistance in times of troubles (verses 1-4), reinforced with a statement of his lifelong trust in the Lord (verses 5–8). These verses are full of wonderful expressions of trust and faith: "You have been my hope ... my confidence since my youth" (verse 5); "From my birth I have relied on You ... I will ever praise you" (verse 6); "You are my strong refuge. My mouth is filled with Your praise, declaring Your splendour all day long" (verses 7b-8). These are the prayers of a man of mature faith, whose response when faced with difficulties is to rely on the Lord.

The psalmist continued with a plea for help in his current troubles (verses 9-13) – it seems that despite his old age he is still facing enemies. But this plea is relatively brief, and mainly the prompt for another outpouring of faith and praise. It is noticeable that unlike in many of the other petitioning psalms, in this psalm the time the psalmist spends describing his predicament is much shorter than the space he devotes to expressions of faith and praise.

Two other points stand out for me in this psalm. Firstly, the psalmist has clearly studied the Scriptures deeply over his life – this psalm frequently quotes other psalms; and secondly, he is keen to pass this learning and his love of

God on to the next generation (verse 18). What an excellent and God-fearing desire – if we know and love the Lord, we should always seek to pass that knowledge on to those that come after us.

Sunday, 24 May 2020

A quiet Sunday, and we enjoy the last Sunday lunch as a foursome before Sam and Ellen's move to Putney. The weather is sunny and bright and we eat on the patio – very pleasant.

More international news, as more and more EU countries are tentatively opening their borders and restarting their tourist industries. But it is noticeable that several are doing so only for other EU citizens, and UK tourists are being pointedly excluded. Whether this is because we are leaving the EU or because the pandemic is further from being under control in this country is not clear, but as this becomes more widely known it is bound to be unpopular and may generate a backlash against the government and its handling of things.

Psalm 72:
The glorious reign of the perfect king

Good morning. Today's psalm is titled "Of Solomon" and, although there is some debate amongst the commentaries as to whether it was a psalm by David for his son Solomon, or by Solomon for his own son Rehoboam, the opening verses seem to be clear enough, as the psalmist prays that the king's son will be granted righteousness and will rule wisely and justly, so that "in his days the righteous will flourish, prosperity will abound till the moon is no more" (verse 7).

A simple enough prayer; in a time of absolute monarchy, the personal character of the king really did matter, as the benefits that flowed from the rule of a good king and the hardships and disasters from an evil one shaped his subjects' lives. The psalmist then goes on, however, to describe the great power of the coming king and the wonderful benefits of his reign in such glowing terms that it slowly becomes clear that he cannot be talking about an earthly king of Israel.

Indeed by the time we reach verse 17: "May His name endure for ever and ever, may it continue as long as the sun. All nations will be blessed through Him, and they will call Him blessed", there is no longer any doubt – this is a Messianic psalm, looking forward to the glorious reign of the Christ the King. And then as we look back over the psalm from the vantage point of the end, we see that *all* of it refers to Jesus.

And we can then join the psalmist in his ringing doxology in verses 18-19: "Praise be to the Lord God, the God of Israel, who alone does marvellous deeds. Praise be to His glorious name forever; may the whole earth be filled with His glory. Amen and Amen".

Amen and Amen indeed.

Monday, 25 May 2020

The last of the four spring bank holidays and, extraordinarily, all four have been glorious days. Unheard of, and very frustrating for everyone as we cannot travel much to the beauty spots! We have a quiet day at home instead with an excellent barbecue in the garden ...

The Prime Minister is in trouble over his special adviser Dominic Cummings, who flouted the lockdown rules in April, several times we gather. The British media in sanctimonious mode is an awesome sight, and one thing that is bound to set them off is the elite not themselves obeying the rules they force on the rest of us.

Psalm 73:
It is good to be near God

Good morning. Today we start Book III of the Book of Psalms. The division of the psalms into five sections or "books" is ancient and traditional, though there is no very clear difference between them, and it may just be that physical scrolls could not conveniently go beyond a certain size and the Book of Psalms required five scrolls (the same reasoning may explain why Samuel, Kings and Chronicles come in two books).

Whatever the reason, as well as the start of Book III, today's psalm is the first of a run of psalms by Asaph, who we met for the first time in Psalm 50. His style is more contemplative, less direct than David's, and in this psalm he meditates on a question that has often worried the faithful: the apparent prosperity and carefree life of the ungodly. Asaph not only reflects on why this is so, but is concerned that it will dismay the God-fearing and cause their faith to weaken.

Indeed even Asaph himself is made to wonder about the role of God in this life – in verses 13-14 he asks "Surely in vain I have kept my heart pure and have washed my hands in innocence. All day long I have been afflicted, and every morning brings new punishments". But then he returns to the Lord (verses 16-17) and is reassured: "When I tried to understand all this, it troubled me deeply till I entered the sanctuary of God; then I understood their final destiny". And he realises (verse 24) that "You guide me with your counsel, and afterward You will take me into glory".

This is a psalm of much soul-searching, but after deep thought and prayer Asaph is able to declare (verse 28) "But as for me, it is good to be near God. I have made the Sovereign Lord my refuge".

Tuesday, 26 May 2020

The Prime Minister announces further relaxations of the lockdown, with more businesses restarting, more shops allowed to open from 15 June, and more freedom to meet others such as family members. It is not obvious what new news has prompted this, and the suspicion grows that the Government is "leading from behind", as adherence to the lockdown rules frays and people are assuming greater liberties anyway. Either that, or it is a smokescreen designed to distract us from the ongoing Cummings affair.

Either way, it smacks of weak government – not a good sign, and Johnson's popularity is sliding fast.

Psalm 74:
Calling on God from the depths of despair

Good morning. We continue with another psalm attributed to Asaph, though it is more likely, given the description of the destruction of the temple, that this psalm was written much later, perhaps after the fall of Jerusalem and the start of the Babylonian captivity.

The psalm is in the form of a lament, and a call to God to remember His people. The first 11 verses of this psalm are among the most anguished in the Psalms; the physical destruction and distress is painful enough for the psalmist but, even more, he feels that Israel has been abandoned by God (verse 9a: "We are given no miraculous signs; no prophets are left"). This opening part culminates in a great cry of "How long?" (verses 9b-11: "None of us knows how long this will be. How long will the enemy mock You, God? Will the foe revile Your name forever? Why do You hold back Your hand?")

But then the tone changes, as the psalmist recalls God's past works for His people (verses 12-17), and feels emboldened enough to plead for God to remember and once again rescue them (verses 18-23).

There is much emotion in this psalm, and more direct language than in most. There is a notable absence of praise, or of thanks. But what comes out for me most is the deep faith behind it, the determination of the psalmist to hold fast to God and rely on God even in the depths of his despair.

Wednesday, 27 May 2020

More and more businesses are re-opening, and today I return to the garage that looks after our cars. My car has developed a weak battery in the weeks of little use, and I am pleased to see they are open again and can deal with it with a full charge overnight. The manager has grown a beard during the lockdown, as so many men seem to have tried to do; his is better than most! I have not myself been remotely tempted …

Although life is indeed returning, it is not returning to "normal". Queues at shops, screens to protect everyone from cashiers to bus drivers, two-metre social distancing markings everywhere, a much greater use of internet shopping and home delivery for all sorts of items. But it is the invisible scars as well: the concern with potentially contaminated surfaces and the constant washing of hands, the ugliness and inconvenience of facemasks – one suddenly realises how much of human interaction is through watching facial expressions, the lack of easy assembly and physical contact, the distrust of people one does not know lest they might be a carrier of the disease. These will take time to overcome.

Psalm 75:
God the Judge will act in His own time

Good morning. In some ways today's psalm, another attributed to Asaph, is a counterbalance to yesterday's. In Psalm 74 we saw an anguished cry to God "Where are You, why will You not act?"; here, in contrast, there is a recognition that God will indeed act, but in His own time.

The theme of "Why do the wicked prosper, when O God will you punish them?" is a common one in the psalms. Here the sin that the psalmist particularly identifies is pride, and self-aggrandisement. The psalmist warns the proud of God's displeasure (verse 4: "To the arrogant I say, 'Boast no more,' and to the wicked, 'Do not lift up your horns'") and states that only God can give true status (verses 6-7: "No one from the east or the west or from the desert can exalt themselves. It is God who judges: He brings one down, he exalts another"). God's judgment on the proud is assured.

But when? The key verse for me is verse 2: "You say 'I choose the appointed time; it is I who judge uprightly'". Impatience is a very human emotion, from children who ask from the back of the car "Are we there yet?" to society at large as we "want it all and want it now". Just as children cannot easily understand the timescale of adult life, so we struggle to comprehend the timescale of God's creation. This psalm is a great antidote to this; it is a psalm of patience, of trust in God as the final judge and the arbiter of the right time to bring His judgment on the world.

I read this psalm and relax – God will act, at His appointed time.

Thursday, 28 May 2020

We complete the vegetable planting in the garden and look forward to a crop later this summer of tomatoes, runner beans, beetroot, cucumbers and courgettes. After looking empty and neglected a month ago, the garden is coming back to life.

Another reawakening – football's Premier League announces it will restart in three weeks. The absence of professional sport has been one of the hallmarks of the lockdown; people seem to be divided between those for whom this is absolutely devastating … and those who are supremely indifferent. But even when it does come back, spectators are likely to be banned, making for empty stadiums and strange atmospheres. Though followers of county cricket at least may not notice much difference!

Psalm 76:
God's presence and power

Good morning. We continue in our run of psalms attributed to Asaph with a psalm today written to celebrate a specific military event, in which Israel has triumphed over an invading force. Some commentators identify this enemy as the Assyrian army led by King Sennacherib, which was repulsed in 701 BC (the story is told in 2 Kings 18-19).

The psalmist makes three separate statements about God in this psalm. He starts by celebrating because God is with His people, His name is known and His presence is felt (verse 2: "His tent is in Salem, His dwelling-place in Zion"). This nearness to God, the immediacy and reality of the relationship between God and His people, is a strong feature of this psalm.

Asaph continues in the main body of the psalm (verses 4-9) with a description of God's victory over Israel's enemies. The victory over the Assyrians (if indeed this was the occasion of the psalm) was a remarkable triumph over a much superior force, and the psalmist is in no doubt of God's power and attributes the victory entirely to His hand.

And finally (verses 10-12), the psalm ends with a call to praise and fear the Lord for His majesty and dominion over all people. Asaph's style throughout this psalm is direct, using short, clear sentences, and this closing section is no exception, for example verse 11a: "Make vows to the Lord your God and fulfil them". One can almost hear him saying to the people "Which bit of this do you not understand?"

This is a psalm with three simple themes: God is with us, God is for us, God is over us. What more can we ask for?

Friday, 29 May 2020

A quieter day, which enables me to catch up on my executor duties for Vicky's mother. Her estate is far from complex but even so I am pleasantly surprised by how much better the process has become online compared to five years ago when I was doing my parents' estates. Even the banks are helpful and easy to speak to.

Sam and Ellen's last evening with us before they move to their flat in Putney and they pack up the "home office" in our dining room very efficiently. After two months of busy clutter It suddenly looks rather empty!

Psalm 77:
From darkness and despair to the calm of the dawn

Good morning. As we continue to read the psalms of Asaph, his style is becoming more familiar. Once again he is writing in short sentences with a directness and clarity, and he is not afraid to raise awkward questions.

Here in today's psalm he is deeply troubled. In the opening section (verses 1-6) he turns to God, but this does not at first comfort him. He persists with his prayers deep into the night, keeping his focus on God, but if anything this increases his despair: he knows God must be hearing his prayer, but he cannot discern an answer. His agony leads to a set of six questions (verses 7-9), questions that Israel so often asked in times of difficulty: "Where are You God? Have You abandoned us for ever?"

Then in verses 10-12 there is a shift in emphasis, as the psalmist decides to cease his focus on his own despair and concentrate instead on the Lord and His mighty deeds. And for the rest of the psalm, the psalmist recalls God's holiness (verses 13-15) and His past rescue of His people (verses 16-20, which recall the Exodus).

The psalm ends quite abruptly; there is no clear indication that this meditation on the Lord has raised Asaph's spirits, no closing hymn of praise as there might have been in a psalm by David. But the change of tone in the psalm suggests that Asaph has indeed passed from the darkness to the dawn, and the lesson of this psalm for me is that, while there is certainly a time in our prayers for telling God about our troubles, there is a greater need to tell ourselves about God's greatness.

Saturday, 30 May 2020

A busy day as we help Sam and Ellen move into their flat in Putney. There is a minor hitch as the previous tenants have not cleared all their possessions from the kitchen (we strongly suspect they had no further need for them and simply couldn't be bothered to take them to the tip) but other than that the day goes really well, with everything moved from Laburnum and from the self-storage very smoothly. It is a lovely flat, clean and in excellent condition, and in a surprisingly quiet road despite being right by Putney High Street.

I even have time to complete the probate application for Vicky's mother. The government's online system is somewhat longwinded but, given how complex the whole question of probate and inheritance tax can be, it is remarkably easy to navigate through. Now I await the grant of probate itself – the website warns that the Court "aims to grant this within four weeks, but due to COVID-19 grants are taking considerably longer to be processed". I wonder how much longer ...

Psalm 78:
Lessons from history, teaching for the future

Good morning. Having extolled Asaph's brevity and concise style over the last two psalms, we come today to the second longest psalm in the Bible. Psalm 78 is a psalm of teaching, as Asaph lists the history of God's deeds and interactions with Israel. The focus is on two aspects of Israel's history in particular: firstly, God's rescue of His people out of Egypt; and secondly, the failure of the tribe of Ephraim, whose leadership of Israel was ended by God when they proved rebellious and ungodly, and He chose the tribe of Judah, and David, to lead Israel in their place.

By telling these two stories the psalmist has two purposes, both of which he summarises at the start of the psalm. They are to *instruct* and to *warn*. The importance of teaching the next generation is central, as verses 2-4 declare: "I will utter … things our ancestors have told us. We will not hide them from their descendants; we will tell the next generation the praiseworthy deeds of the Lord, His power, and the wonders He has done".

And the reason we should do so is explained in verses 7-8: "Then they would put their trust in God and would not forget His deeds but would keep His commands. They would not be like their ancestors – a stubborn and rebellious generation, whose hearts were not loyal to God, whose spirits were not faithful to Him".

Passing on our knowledge of the Lord to our children, so that they may come to know and love Him too, is one of our most sacred obligations. The *history* in this psalm is both familiar and at the same time perhaps somewhat remote from us; the *teaching* from the psalm is as relevant today as it was when Asaph wrote it.

Sunday, 31 May 2020

Day two of Sam and Ellen's move and a longer day, as they have to drive to Camden to pack up all of Ellen's things in her previous flat, largely from scratch. But after much effort they succeed, and late in the day we join them to complete the unloading into their new flat. A most successful two days for them.

Bad news as our bread machine breaks. It is an awkward time to try to buy a new one as no-one has any in stock! It seems that one of the things Lockdown Britain decided to do when we were all confined to home was bake bread, and (along with shops having no flour) every supplier of bread machines was cleaned out.

Psalm 79:
Retribution for those who take the Lord's name in vain

Good morning. Today's psalm is a very similar to Psalm 74, and continues the soul-searching of the faithful after the fall of Jerusalem in 586 BC. It has three parts – like Psalm 74, it starts with a lament for the fate of Jerusalem (verses 1-4), and then moves to the main body of the psalm with a call to God to act (verses 5 12), but then, unlike Psalm 74, the psalmist ends with a promise of praise (verse 13). The psalm is less anguished than Psalm 74, and more considered, but there is no doubt of the pain the psalmist feels.

Two things stand out for me in this psalm. The first is that the disaster has not estranged the psalmist from God or destroyed his faith. Despite his anger and despair, he is not turning against God but turning to Him. Nor does he ask God why the disaster has occurred, but merely how long His people will have to go on suffering. There is a strong faith and commitment to God behind this psalm.

And the second is how the prayer for God to act revolves around three separate themes. As well as the familiar themes of enjoining God to punish Israel's oppressors (verses 6-7), and show mercy and forgiveness to Israel itself (verses 8 and 11), He is lastly called on to act to glorify His name (verses 9-10).

We have lost a lot of the feeling of the power of God's name in our modern society; even believers routinely misuse it. But the Lord's name was always considered holy by Israel, enough so to be the subject of the Third Commandment: "You shall not take the name of the Lord your God in vain".

In this prayer, Asaph is asking God to judge those who have taken His name in vain, and show the world that it is worthy of praise.

Monday, 1 June 2020

A big day for the country as primary schools start to reopen. Only for some of their pupils, and attendance is patchy at best but, whatever their parents may think, and despite the concerns and opposition of the teachers' unions (alas more political than practical), the children seem to enjoy it.

A big day for us too as an internet hunt for a new bread machine last night is finally successful ... and Vicky goes to pick it up this morning! Very efficient indeed, under 24 hours from one machine breaking to the next one being ordered, bought and brought home.

Psalm 80:
A plea for restoration to God's favour

Good morning. This morning we have another psalm in which prayers are offered to God beseeching Him to return to His defeated people, and to restore them to His favour. Unusually, the prayers are on behalf of the Northern Kingdom, Israel, perhaps after its defeat by Assyria in 722 BC.

This psalm is a poem full of beautiful imagery. The psalmist starts by calling on the Lord as the Shepherd of Israel; this is a familiar image for us but rare in the Book of Psalms – the only other psalm to refer to God as the Shepherd is Psalm 23, "The Lord is my Shepherd". The main body of the psalm (verses 8-16) likens Israel to a vine, planted and nurtured by God; again a familiar image, and it reminds us that of all plants, the vine needs more care and tending than most to prosper and bring forth good fruit, and is more susceptible to damage and loss of fruit if neglected. Perhaps there is also a recognition that the vigneron has from time to time to prune the vine very deeply if it is to grow strong.

The main prayer in the psalm is repeated three times, in verses 3, 7 and 19; each time the psalmist prays with increased urgency and emotion as he calls first on God, then God Almighty (or God of Hosts in some translations), then Lord God Almighty, the last being *Yahweh*, the Covenant name for God and the most sacred way of calling upon Him.

But in among these appeals to Israel's God, there is also a call for God to bring forth a man to lead the people back to Him – verse 17: "Let Your hand rest on the man at Your right hand, the son of man You have raised up for Yourself".

The psalmist's original listeners will have heard this primarily as a call for a God-fearing king to lead His people; but we can see it as a prophetic call for the Messiah to come to our rescue – and in this light, we are reminded (verse 18) of our part: "Then we will not turn away from You; revive us, and we will call on Your name".

God will rescue us. But in return we must not again turn away.

Tuesday, 2 June 2020

A quieter day at home. We continue the project of restoring the garden to its full early summer glory, as we start to get the pots on the patio ready for planting. Although the timing of the lockdown has in many ways been fortunate, with fine weather to lift spirits and allow us to enjoy sitting in the garden, we are rather behind with the usual spring busy-ness as garden centres were closed for so long.

Nationally, the easing of the restrictions has had two effects: the black-and-white certainty of the early days of the lockdown has given way to shades of grey and confusion, as no-one is really sure what we are now allowed to do and what is safe; and other news, so long relegated to a brief mention on the inside pages by the all-dominating news of the virus, is once again taking its place on the front pages. The end of this month sees an important deadline in the negotiations with the EU on future trade arrangements and, as things stand, the talks appear to be going very badly. Plus ça change … Perhaps we will in time look back on the three months from March to May as a blessed period when at least we did not have to hear endlessly about Brexit!

Psalm 81:
God's longing for His people to listen to Him

Good morning. The glorious variety of the Book of Psalms, with psalms of prayer, penitence and praise following each other almost, it seems, at random, gives us today a celebration psalm, probably for use at the Feast of Tabernacles, when the Jews remember their time in the wilderness after the Exodus.

Public worship with music was an integral part of the Jewish faith – there is a tradition that the custom of singing and music was instigated by David after he had brought the Ark to Jerusalem – and the first part of this psalm (verses 1-5) is a summons to the people to sing to the Lord. But the Feast of Tabernacles was also a time for the people to be instructed about their God and, in the rest of this psalm, it is God Himself who speaks to them.

God first of all briefly reminds them that He rescued them from Egypt (verses 6-7), and then recites part of the Law. This is a call to obedience, a reminder of the duty of listening to God's Word. But the psalm then turns into a lament by God (verses 11-16) that Israel will not listen. Surprisingly, at this point there are no threats to Israel, no warnings from God of the price of not heeding His call. Instead there is just deep sadness, a longing that they would return to Him so He could once again nurture them.

When I was young I feared my father's anger – there were times when he was properly cross with me. But far worse was when he would simply say, sadly, "I am so disappointed". Here, the people of Israel are told of God's great disappointment.

What a crushing rebuke this must have been, what a call to return to the Lord.

Wednesday, 3 June 2020

A much cooler day today, grey and overcast. And even a little rain – not enough, alas, and after our extremely dry May (the driest and sunniest on record) we have already begun to get the first mentions of water shortages and hosepipe bans in the press. It is quite extraordinary given the rain in February, when much of the country was suffering from very bad floods.

We go again to the garden centre and buy a selection of plants for our pots and boxes on the patio. The queues are less, but the selection is not that good (the vegetable selection is very poor, so as well that we concentrated on them first). It does not stop us filling two whole trolleys, so much planting ahead of us!

Psalm 82:
God the righteous and just Judge

Good morning. Again the magnificent variety in the Book of Psalms greets us, as today the psalmist turns to God for help over corrupt and unjust judges. The problem of incomplete or unfair justice was a real one, not least because there was no earthly remedy if the legal system treated one badly, and the only recourse of the righteous was to appeal to God, whose justice is complete. This is not the first psalm we have met on this theme, as David called on God in similar words in Psalm 58.

Here the psalmist pictures God sitting in judgment over the judges (called "gods" in verses 1 and 6, in Hebrew *Elohim*, perhaps because they exercise God-given authority on earth), and calling them to account. God accuses them (verse 2; the word you is plural here, so refers to the judges), tells them what their duties are and how they should have behaved (verses 3-5), and then delivers His verdict upon them (verses 6-7). The psalmist, having painted this scene for us, then closes by calling on God to carry it through and judge the whole earth.

In this short psalm, the psalmist turns to God when human justice fails, and comforts himself with the knowledge that God's justice is both inexorable and righteous. What a great comfort to know that in the Heavenly Court we are assured a fair hearing and a just verdict.

Thursday, 4 June 2020

Another cooler day, and we complete the planting of the flowers we bought the previous day. A good thing it is not as hot, as it is a much longer task than we expected; we rather overbought and have more than enough flowers for all our pots and boxes, and some left over for the flowerbeds! But it stays dry, even though much of the rest of the country is getting rain.

National politics continues its slow return to normality, though the first vote through the lobbies at Westminster after the remote sessions of recent months takes on a farcical look with a queue over half a mile long of MPs, all two metres from each other, waiting to vote. The process takes over an hour and, really, there has to be a better way in the 21st century of parliament expressing its views!

More successfully, Sir Keir Starmer, the leader of the opposition, is finding his feet well in the weekly Prime Minister's Questions sessions. He has a difficult balancing act between supporting the efforts of the government to control the pandemic and holding them to account, and he will not please everyone, but he seems to be getting it about right and is effective at exposing the government's inconsistencies.

Psalm 83: A call to God for help against many enemies

Good morning. We come to the last of the psalms by Asaph, and today he calls upon God for aid as Israel's enemies mass against her. The psalm is in two parts: after a brief prayer calling on God to act, the psalmist describes (verses 2-8) the magnitude of the assault on Israel – it seems that all of her neighbours have combined to attack and annihilate her, and then (verses 9-16) petitions God for His help in overcoming them. Finally the psalm closes with the hope that, in crushing Israel's enemies, God will become known and acknowledged as the true God, the Most High over all the earth.

For much of the historical section of the Old Testament – Judges, Samuel, Kings, Chronicles – Israel seems to be at war with its neighbours, and this psalm, with its long litany of those enemies, makes me think why this was so, why Israel aroused such hostility. And the message of the Bible is that in a world where people believed in many gods, the Israelites were uncomfortable neighbours; instead of conforming to the diplomatic belief of the day that "there are many gods; our god is for us, your god is for you", they loudly proclaimed "there is one God; our God is true, your god is false". No wonder Israel's neighbours objected.

Today Christians face a different but not unrelated challenge, especially in the post-religious West. In a world where most people now believe there is no god, we proclaim that on the contrary there is a God, and He does matter. And in a real sense, unless we are as beset by enemies as Israel was at the time of this psalm, we are not proclaiming it loudly or effectively enough.

We should therefore echo Asaph's final verse, the last of his prayers in his 12 psalms: "Let them know that You, whose name is the Lord – that You alone are the Most High over all the earth".

Friday, 5 June 2020

The downside of internet shopping today, as an alarm clock I ordered arrived – and is immediately thrown away as it has a very loud and intrusive tick. Very difficult to sleep through, and I wonder why people make things so obviously not fit for purpose? Frustrating, and I resume the internet search for a replacement.

The papers are full of introspection on the stubborn daily death rate in the UK: on one day earlier this week, more people died in the UK than in the whole of the EU-27. Nobody can really explain why, least of all, it seems, the government.

Psalm 84:
Longing to be with God

Good morning. In today's psalm we have a sense of the deep longing of the faithful for God. The psalm follows a pilgrim on his way to Jerusalem to worship at the Temple, and his joy at the thought of what awaits him at journey's end.

We know that God is everywhere, that we can meet Him at any time and in any place. But there is still something inspiring for us about holy places, churches and cathedrals. So it was for the Israelites – they knew that God was present throughout the world, but even so Jerusalem was special, and the Temple even more so. And so our psalmist is full of excitement at the thought of being in the Temple (verses 1-4), at being able to worship God there.

This expectation mounts as he makes his pilgrimage (verses 5-8), even though the journey goes through the barren lands of the Valley of Baca. Finally he arrives, and rejoices; the journey is over and worthwhile (verse 10: "Blessed is one day in Your courts than a thousand elsewhere") and he concludes by expressing his joy in a final verse of praise, verse 12: "O Lord Almighty, blessed is the man who trusts in You".

For me, the yearning for God and the joy at being in His presence come through every verse of this lovely psalm.

Saturday, 6 June 2020

The relaxations of the lockdown restrictions have had one interesting consequence: there is once again a discernible difference in the traffic past our house at the weekend. At the height of the lockdown there was hardly any traffic on our road whatever day of the week it was, but now the weekdays at least are more busy.

The easing continues with further announcements of businesses allowed to reopen. One senses that the economic need to restart the economy and commerce is weighing ever more heavily on the decisions the government is making. That, and perhaps also the fact that in London, at least, there are now very few new infections – this should not sway the government but the London-centric nature of Whitehall is well known!

But still no sign of churches reopening for communal worship; as large indoor gatherings they are deemed a high-risk environment, so we will have to wait longer to share the joy of today's psalm! (Though with the size of most rural congregations these days, social distancing inside the church would sadly not be much of a problem).

Another day of quite heavy rain at times; very good for the garden, which certainly needs it, and we are pleased we managed to complete the planting of all our flowers earlier in the week.

Psalm 85:
A prayer for renewal and restoration

Good morning. Today's psalm is a plea for renewal and a return to God's favour. The psalm is thought by many commentators to date from the time of the return from Exile; the returning Israelites would have faced a daunting rebuilding task, and the psalmist starts (verses 1-3) by remembering God's past mercies to Israel, previous times when He has restored His people, and asks (verses 4-7) for Him to restore them again.

The second part of the psalm (verses 8-13) gives God's response; it is not in the form of direct divine speech (as, for example, we saw in Psalm 46), but uses a style common in the Old Testament for relaying the Word of the Lord as reported speech: "I will listen to what the Lord God will say".

And what beautiful poetry it is too. Verses 10-11 paint a picture of a world in harmony with God: "Love and faithfulness meet together; righteousness and peace kiss each other. Faithfulness springs forth from the earth, and righteousness looks down from heaven", and the psalmist closes confident that "The Lord will indeed give what is good".

The pivot of the psalm for me is the heartfelt prayer in verses 6-7: "Will You not revive us again, that Your people may rejoice in You? Show us Your unfailing love, Lord, and grant us Your salvation". "Grant us Your salvation" – God's people's need for forgiveness and restoration to His favour is a theme running through much of the Old Testament, and is as true of our life today. With good reason do we echo this prayer in the Responses in Morning and Evening Prayer: "O Lord, show Your mercy upon us; And grant us Your salvation".

Sunday, 7 June 2020

A quiet day, with little to disturb our Sunday. I make use of the sunny morning to spend a couple of hours pruning the roses; almost as if as a reward, the heavens open in the afternoon and the garden receives more heavy and very welcome rain.

The newspapers report just 77 deaths from the virus in the last 24 hours. Reported deaths are always lower at the weekend for some reason (perhaps it is due to the paperwork not being done, as one presumes it isn't the virus observing the Sabbath), but even so this is the first time since before the lockdown started that the figure has been under 100. The trend is definitely lower, even if more slowly than we would all like.

Psalm 86:
A devoted servant calls on his Master

Good morning. Psalm 86 is marked as "A prayer of David" – this is an unusual designation, with only four other psalms called "a prayer" in their title. It is less structured than many of David's psalms, more an outpouring of his soul to God.

Although the psalm does contain verses of praise and adoration (for example, verses 8-10), it is mainly a psalm marked by repeated requests. Several times in these requests David calls God by the less common name *Adonai*, best translated here perhaps as Master, and refers to himself as His servant. David bases his prayers on this relationship as, although in any master-servant relationship the servant is clearly inferior, he is not without any rights at all and David feels he can ask his Master for benevolent and merciful treatment.

In total, there are more than a dozen times that David makes a direct plea for God to act: Hear me, Answer me, Guard my life, Have mercy on me, Bring me joy, Hear my prayer, Listen to my cry, Teach me, Give me an undivided heart, Turn to me, Have mercy on me (again), Grant Your strength to me, Save me, Give me a sign of Your goodness.

Many of these prayers are asking God to act out of His mercy for David's sake, but two, both in verse 11, stand out for me as slightly different, as David asks "Teach me Your way, O Lord, and I will walk in Your truth; give me an undivided heart, that I may fear Your name". Even though David knows the Lord and has studied His way, he still asks to be guided further, so that he can perfect his relationship with God and hold ever more closely to Him.

What a reminder to us all to continue diligently our studies of God's Word.

Monday, 8 June 2020

Another day of lower death tolls, just 55. But before we celebrate too much, the news from New Zealand puts it in perspective – they have had no deaths now for over a fortnight and no longer even have any cases of the virus. The government there is lifting the final lockdown restrictions; even sports grounds are open to crowds. Only their ban on foreigners visiting the country (imposed very early and rigidly applied with no exceptions at all) remains; for once their position so far from everywhere has helped them!

The cold snap continues – a considerable contrast to May, which was the hottest and sunniest May ever.

Psalm 87:
Zion city of God

Good morning. Today we have a psalm from the Sons of Korah, which looks forward to Zion, the New Jerusalem that God has created as the eternal home of His faithful. It is a short psalm, but the psalmists pack a lot into it.

We hear how God has founded His city (verse 1) and loves it (verse 2), we hear how its fame has already spread (verse 3), and how even Israel's enemies will one day acknowledge the Lord as sovereign (verses 4-6; *Rahab*, in verse 4, is here a name for Egypt, not the woman who helped Joshua's spies at Jericho). And finally (verse 7), the psalmists turn to the community of those living in Zion – they will make music and sing that "All my fountains are in You", all their blessings flow from God.

Verse 3 of the psalm was the inspiration for John Newton's great hymn "Glorious things of thee are spoken. Zion city of our God". The hymn ends with the contrast between earthly riches and the lasting joy that awaits the people of God:

Fading is the worldling's pleasure,
all his boasted pomp and show;
solid joys and lasting treasure
none but Zion's children know.

In this psalm I sense God's love for the Eternal City, and for those who dwell in it. St John's glorious description of the New Jerusalem in Revelation is much longer and more detailed, but the simplicity of this psalm has its own power.

Tuesday, 9 June 2020

An introduction to the new world of hospitals today, as Vicky's father has to go to Guildford Hospital for some treatment. Vicky takes him, and has a precise arrival time – she must not only not be late, but she cannot be early either. She is not allowed into the building but leaves him with the medical staff at the door. And the same on collection – she is given a precise time to be there, and waits in her car as he is brought out.

He comes to stay with us for the night to recover, our first visitor (apart from Sam and Ellen) since March. We are not entirely clear whether the general lockdown rules, let alone the "isolation for seniors" rules, allow this, but it is on the direct orders of the hospital, who say he has to be looked after overnight – in more normal times he would have probably spent the night in the hospital itself, but that is something they prefer to avoid if possible these days. So it must be OK, and it is good to see him again.

Psalm 88:
A prayer from the depths of despair

Good morning. Our psalm this morning is a lamentation, and one of the most unremittingly melancholy, if not outright bleak, of all the 150 psalms. The psalmist is clearly in deep distress; it seems he has been suffering, perhaps from an illness or an injury, for much of his life and fears he is now near death, and the psalm does not contain any uplifting element or even, it seems, any hope.

For all this, the psalmist continues to pray to the Lord. He may feel that God has abandoned him and turned His back on him (verse 14: "Why, O Lord, do You reject me and hide Your face from me?"), but he continues to pray; indeed he calls on God every day (verses 1 and 9).

It is hard to extract much joy from this psalm. It is in every sense a catalogue of suffering and woe. But from beginning to end, there is no bitterness or anger directed towards God, and only just the one direct question of God's response to the psalmist's needs – verse 14, as we have already noted. Instead there is a recognition of the sovereignty of God, who decrees all things. In this, the psalm is perhaps most similar to the Book of Job, another great study of suffering.

We wonder why the God of goodness and light allows innocent people to suffer – it is one of the questions, almost accusations, most often levelled by non-Christians. The message of this psalm, for me, is that we may never know why, it may not be for us to know – but instead we should concentrate on and be satisfied with knowing the God who knows why.

Wednesday, 10 June 2020

Vicky's father is in good form in the morning and she takes him home; but later he is suffering again and taken back into hospital, this time by ambulance, and this time to spend the night in their care.

We have a rather different family video meeting this evening, as we all follow our daughter's instructions to cook exactly the same food – Nepali "momos" or meat dumplings, a bit like dim sum. They are delicious, and it is great fun to be making them all together, albeit in four different households.

The news is full of riots and unrest as the UK part of the "Black Lives Matter" movement latches onto the death of a black man in the States at the hands of the police (a genuinely appalling story), and turns it into an assault on past historical racial injustices like slavery. One wonders quite how genuine the anger is (most of the rioters are white) or how productive (there are more current racial injustices to address); it is perhaps more a sign that the underlying frustrations with the restrictions of lockdown are beginning to boil over.

Psalm 89:
God's everlasting covenant

Good morning. Today's psalm is a long contemplation of the challenge facing God's faithful in the latter years of Israel's decline – how to reconcile the eternal and unchanging nature of God's promise to Israel to protect and prosper His chosen people, with the psalmist's present day reality of decline and decay.

The psalm is unusual in that, unlike the many psalms that start with complaint and petitions for help and end with praise and joy, here the psalmist starts by recalling God's former great works with praise and joy, but then (verses 38-45), with an unusually abrupt change of tone, laments that Israel's current situation is much less happy, and that God seems to have withdrawn his favours.

The earnestness of the search to understand this apparent suspension of God's covenant is shown in the length and detail of the first section of the psalm, where the gifts showered on King David are recalled in glowing terms. The psalmist concentrates particularly on the eternal nature of God's promise – verse 35 is a remarkable statement, "Once for all, I have sworn by My holiness – and I will not lie to David" – and this makes his confusion at Israel's current state even greater.

But despite this apparent abandonment, the psalmist does not cease his prayers, and the psalm closes (verses 46-51) with repeated pleas for God to remember Israel again. It is this that I will take away from this psalm – after his long meditation on the woes that Israel is suffering, in the closing verses all the psalmist's anger is spent and there is no recrimination against God, just a trust in Him and a plea that He will once again remember His people.

Thursday, 11 June 2020

Vicky's father is still in hospital and likely to be kept in for a few days, as he has some of the symptoms of pneumonia. In these days of the virus he is duly also tested for COVID-19; there are mixed messages and they seem unable either to confirm or deny whether he has it. We are not told to self-isolate, but decide to get a fortnight's supply of food in just in case they change their mind. We also decide to sleep in separate bedrooms – it would be better if we did not both get ill together – and I thereby become the first person to sleep on the new spare bed we bought in March, just before the lockdown. It is perfectly OK but not quite as comfortable as our main bed!

Psalm 90: The eternal nature of God

Good morning. At the start of Book IV of the Book of Psalms, we have a psalm entitled "A prayer of Moses, the man of God". It is the only psalm in the Psalter attributed to him and perhaps therefore the oldest psalm of them all. It seems to come from towards the end of the Israelites' journeys in the Wilderness, and Moses is both looking back on God's protection during those years and forward to the Promised Land.

In this psalm Moses describes the eternal nature of God, with the beautiful poetry of verse 2: "Before the mountains were born or You brought forth the earth and the world, from everlasting to everlasting You are God", and compares it with the frail and transient nature of man. After the Exodus, Moses would have been fully aware of how dependent on God the Israelites were and, as he saw a generation pass away in the Wilderness, he will have witnessed God's judgment first hand.

But the psalm does not end there, as the closing third, from verse 11 onwards, is a prayer for the new generation, born in the Wilderness and about to enter the Promised Land. For them, Moses asks for God's love and compassion, and for God to give them work to do and His blessing over it. There is much wisdom in this prayer – it is not for an easy life but a fulfilling one, not for a safe life but one lived with the joy of knowing the Lord.

I conclude that to know the eternal Lord and to do His work – the ambition that Moses had for the people under his care – has stood the test of time, and is as valid for us today as it was over 3,000 years ago.

Friday, 12 June 2020

I spoke too soon yesterday about our new bed as, after just one night, one of the wooden slats has broken. I don't think it was because I was too heavy; rather, it was a badly flawed bit of wood with a huge knot in it and no strength at all. Fortunately the bed company accept that it is fully under guarantee and will send a replacement set of slats, and meanwhile I change to yet another bedroom ...

In the evening, the Phoenix Masters hold a Cocktail Party by Zoom to mark our 4th birthday. It is our first online gathering and the first time most people will have seen each other since our Spring Dinner on 11 March; it is a great success with a large turnout, and the Association seems in excellent heart despite the constraints on physically meeting.

Psalm 91:
God's protective care

Good morning. Today's psalm has neither attribution nor description, so we cannot say when it was written or the circumstances of the author at the time. But that is immaterial, as the message of the psalm is timeless. The theme of the psalm is God's protection for the faithful and their security in His care, a promise that is as valid now as it was for ancient Israel; indeed, with its repeated mentions of pestilence and the plague (verses 3, 6 and in some translations 10) the psalm is both timely and completely appropriate for us today.

The psalm is a reassurance for the faithful. The psalmist starts by declaring God's protection (verse 1: "He who dwells in the shelter of the Most High will rest in the shadow of the Almighty") and adds his personal experience as further reassurance (verse 2: "I will say of the Lord, 'He is my refuge and my fortress, my God, in whom I trust'"). The main part of the psalm (verses 3-13) then details the many ways in which God will protect us if (verse 9) we "make the Most High our dwelling", verses 11 and 12 in particular will sound familiar, as they were quoted by Satan to Jesus during his temptations in the desert (see Matthew 4:6).

The last three verses of the psalm see a change of voice, from the psalmist reassuring us of God's protection to God Himself confirming his care. For me, the key to God's promise is that He does not say "I will make sure nothing even slightly unpleasant happens to you" – that is not the case, as faithful people can suffer in this life – but instead he says "I will rescue you, I will protect you, I will answer you,

I will be with you in trouble, I will deliver you, I will show you My salvation".

For me, this is a remarkable set of pledges, in the first person, and completes a psalm that I find full of reassurance and comfort for those who believe.

Saturday, 13 June 2020

A quieter day at home, with a sunny morning in which we do some more gardening – alas, the weeds and brambles are finding the recent combination of sunshine and rain just as conducive to growing as the flowers and vegetables! – and then a fierce thunderstorm in the evening.

It is anything but quiet in central London, though, with more protests and demonstrations against racism and discrimination. Large crowds (all wholly ignoring the two-metre rule!), and predictably some turn violent – if the virus is still active in London, there will be no better ways to reignite spreading it.

Psalm 92: The joy of praising the Lord

Good morning. Today's psalm has the unusual heading "A song for the Sabbath day", and how appropriate therefore that it falls in our sequence on a Sunday. It is a call to praise the Lord, to rejoice in His manifold and mighty works.

There is a sunny optimism and joy running throughout this psalm; the psalmist has witnessed the Lord's providence and care for His people, and has seen the results. Verses 10 and 11 are explicitly recording facts: "You have exalted my horn … My eyes have seen the defeat of my adversaries", not expressing hopes for future deliverance. Even the reference to the foolish and the wicked (verses 6 and 7) is light, and does not seriously interrupt the overall joyful nature of the psalm.

I love the imagery of the trees in verses 12 and 13. The palm tree was both long lived (in contrast to the wicked, who are "like grass" and wither quickly) and immensely productive well into old age, and the cedar of Lebanon was a huge and very strong tree, growing to a great height. But I also note that they do not grow like that by chance; they are "planted in the house of the Lord" and will "flourish in the courts of our God". So it is with God's faithful people: like the trees the psalmist describes, we are tended, nourished and protected by God, and like the trees we will flourish in the courts of our God.

Sunday, 14 June 2020

The news is better from Vicky's father; he is as cheerful as ever, and they think that they will send him home in the next day or two. Which also probably means that even if the various tests they did on him for COVID-19 were not entirely conclusive, they think it unlikely he has the virus – good news for us too and we can think about easing our self-isolation. Now we just have the matter of all that extra food Vicky laid in to eat our way through!

Psalm 93:
The Lord reigns

Good morning. Today we have the first in a short run of psalms (93, 95-99) concentrating on God as King. The catchphrase of these psalms is "The Lord reigns", and these are the opening words of our psalm today as it starts the sequence.

Despite the shortness of the psalm, the anonymous psalmist manages fully to describe God's reign. It is firmly established, it is strong, it is from the infinite past and it is eternal. He then tries to think of something to compare God's kingdom to, and he chooses a mighty storm at sea, probably the most awesome sight in nature that he can imagine for its power, noise and ferocity – but, he declares, the Lord is mightier even than this.

So far the psalmist has used words that might have been used, with customary sycophantic exaggeration, by many subjects of ancient rulers: in the ancient world it was not unusual for subjects to write flatteringly of their king, proclaiming their power, declaring their kingdom will last for ever. But all such claims were false; all earthly kingdoms fall. The psalmist is keen to declare that this is not the case with God's kingdom, and does so by highlighting two further features of God's rule: that it is *just*, based on statutes, and that it is *holy*. And these distinguish it from that of mere earthly kings, all of which will, despite the protestations, fade away. As the psalm concludes, "Your statutes stand firm; holiness adorns Your house for endless days, O Lord".

I marvel that in five short verses, the psalmist has so captured the essence of God's kingdom – we have here a complete picture of what it means when we declare "The Lord reigns".

Monday, 15 June 2020

General shops were open for the first time today, and the news reports long queues as people take advantage. We are not tempted to join them! Restaurants and bars, however, are still not open (nor are hairdressers and barbers – the wait goes on for my summer haircut!).

Psalm 94:
God the righteous Judge

Good morning. Today we have a psalm on God's justice. Justice is a major theme of the Book of Psalms, with a number of "justice psalms" praising God because He is just, calling on Him to judge the wicked (especially those who oppress Israel), and looking forward to his judgment on and rewards for the righteous.

Today's psalm is addressed to three quite different audiences. The psalmist starts by speaking to God: he declares that God is "the God who avenges", who sees all mankind and will judge righteously, and asks Him to bring vengeance, or judgment, on the wicked, whose deeds are described in verses 3-7. He then changes his attention and speaks to the wicked themselves (verses 8-11), calling them senseless fools for ignoring God and thinking that He will ignore them.

Finally he speaks to his fellow believers, explaining to them firstly (verses 12-15) that their suffering was a necessary disciplining from God, designed not to destroy them but for their benefit, and then closing the psalm with more words of reassurance and comfort that the Lord will protect them and pass judgment on their oppressors.

I find the positioning of this psalm, coming as it does in a run of psalms that celebrate God's kingdom and His rule, very revealing. In the ancient world, with absolute rulers the norm, justice was often withheld and upright honest rulers were rare. And there is little more dispiriting that when justice is denied one. So when the psalmists contemplated

God's eternal kingdom, one feature they looked forward to greatly was righteous justice, delivered by a fair and just ruler.

We can also look forward to God's perfect justice, in our case with the added assurance that because of Christ's sacrifice on the cross, God's judgment will be tempered with mercy.

Tuesday, 16 June 2020

A quieter day at home, as I set up two online whisky tastings and invite friends and family to join them.

New Zealand reported its first case of COVID-19 for over three weeks overnight. It was brought into the country by someone coming from England. What a tragedy that we are likely to be treated by other more advanced and successful countries as a pariah people, carriers of disease and not welcome to visit.

Psalm 95: A call to worship, a sermon from God

Good morning. We have a psalm today that is a microcosm of a religious gathering, whether at the synagogue or the church.

The psalm starts with a summons to sing joyfully to the Lord (verses 1-2). Singing joyfully has been part of man's relationship with God for millennia, and surely this is rightly so, because God wants us to be joyful and has given us so much to be joyful about. We then move on to praise and awe, as the psalm describes God's greatness (verses 3-5) – note that verse 3 proclaims that the Lord is *the* great God, not just *a* great god. And having contemplated God's greatness, the natural response is to kneel and worship Him (verses 6-7a).

The stage is now set for the congregation to be instructed. The speaker and the whole tone of the psalm change as the people listen to the sermon (verses 8-11). And this is a very special sermon, because it is God Himself who speaks to his faithful people. It is a warning, an exhortation not to harden their hearts against God, not to turn away.

Such a direct warning is remarkable, and indeed it is the subject of possibly the oldest bible commentary we still have: Hebrews 3:7 to 4:13 contains a long analysis of God's counsel in this psalm, a unique case of a New Testament commentary at great length on a part of the Old.

Once again we see the timelessness of the psalms: here is a psalm written perhaps 3,000 years ago, considered at length by the writer of Hebrews 2,000 years ago, and still entirely relevant to us today. And how interesting that our style of communual worship – praise, reverence, instruction – has changed so little in that time.

Wednesday, 17 June 2020

A surprise visitor before breakfast, as my brother calls by on his morning bicycle ride. It is 15 miles from his house to ours, but with the still less-than-full traffic it takes him under an hour. We have a suitably socially-distanced coffee in the garden before he sets off home ... and all this before a full day's work.

Premier League football returns this evening – and with it emotion, controversy and even a blatant refereeing error, with a clear goal disallowed. The long march back to normality has taken a further step!

Psalm 96:
Sing praise to God the eternal Ruler

Good morning. We continue in the run of psalms celebrating God's reign; although, like the earlier ones in this little sequence, it is anonymous, it echoes the song of praise that David sang when the Israelites brought the Ark to Jerusalem (1 Chronicles 16), so many commentators ascribe it to David.

The psalm is an invitation to sing to the Lord and praise Him for His rule over the whole earth. The psalm first commands the people of God, then widens the command to all nations, then finally calls on creation itself to acknowledge the Lord – verses 11-12 "Let the heavens rejoice, let the earth be glad, let the sea resound … let the fields be jubilant … the trees of the forest sing for joy". And all because (verse 10) "the Lord reigns".

There is a directness, a straightforwardness about this claim of God's greatness and His infinite rule, which is on the surface difficult to match to the lived experience of the Israelites. Even in the days of King David, Israel was a small and comparatively minor kingdom, often at the mercy of the great empires of their day and sometimes very much at the receiving end of their power. So, to Israel's neighbours, the claims in this psalm would have seemed ridiculous.

But both the psalmist and his listeners understood that their statements of God's kingship were not just about the present but much more about a future reality, something to come when God brings His creation to fruition.

This is therefore above all a Messianic psalm, looking ahead to Christ the Messiah and His eternal rule. Far from presenting a false picture of the earthly reality of Israel at that time, it states a belief about the world to come. We can share in that belief, and therefore with the psalmist we should proclaim loudly among the nations: "The Lord reigns".

Thursday, 18 June 2020

Today marks 80 years since de Gaulle's famous rallying cry on the BBC to the French in June 1940, and we have a visit from President Macron of France to mark it. No 14-day quarantine for him! There is a fly past of RAF and French Air Force planes and, as it was due to go over Richmond Park on its way to central London, I went to see it. Alas they flew quite low, the Park is large, and quite full of trees, and although I certainly heard the planes, I could not see them. But a very pleasant visit to the Park and a good two-mile walk home.

Psalm 97: God's awesome power

Good morning. Our run of psalms celebrating God's sovereignty continues this morning with a three-part psalm considering the greatness of His rule, the response from the people of earth and finally God's care for the faithful. Behind all three parts there is a call to rejoice at the Lord's righteous rule.

The psalms in this little sequence are given the name "Enthronement psalms"; they all declare God's greatness and His complete authority over the earth in similar terms. In today's Enthronement psalm, though, the psalmist chooses to concentrate on one aspect of God's kingship in particular: the awesomeness of His power. Such is His power that the whole earth trembles, the mountains melt like wax before the Lord. The psalmist reminds us of the imagery of God from the Exodus – clouds by day and fire by night – both to describe God's presence but also to re-emphasise this power, a power that we cannot look directly upon.

The human response to such a powerful God is mixed (verses 7-9). His rule will be a matter of joy to the faithful, but it will strike terror into others. Idol-worshippers will be dismayed, and the psalmist declares that both they and also their false gods will be forced to acknowledge God and worship Him. But Israel will rejoice at the coming of God's kingdom.

The psalmist ends with some instruction and encouragement for those who love the Lord (verses 10-12). They will be guarded and protected, light is shed on them, and joy will be in their heart. This picture of the faithful rejoicing in

God's presence is so familiar that we perhaps do not think often enough how surprising it is that we should feel so safe in the hands of one so powerful; the importance of this psalm to me is that it directly reminds me of that power, and assures me that, even so, I should rejoice, and that I have nothing to fear.

Friday, 19 June 2020

The government announces that the "Covid Alert Level" is reduced from 4 to 3, and that the R number (rate of re-infection) is well below 1. Both good news, and the idea, when they were introduced, was that this would be the trigger for some relaxations of the lockdown. That was before politics, and the need for the Prime Minister to recover from the self-inflicted wound of the Cummings affair, intervened – we have had many of the relaxations already and science is, it seems, following not leading political reality!

Psalm 98:
A call to praise the Lord

Good morning. Today's psalm is very similar to the one we had two days earlier, Psalm 96. Both celebrate the coming reign of God on earth and call upon the whole world, all its peoples and indeed all of nature, to rejoice.

There is some evidence that this psalm was written on the return from Exile in Babylon, and verses 1-3 can be seen therefore as a celebration that God has remembered His people and rescued them (the Hebrew word translated in most English versions as "salvation", and used twice in these opening verses, can also mean "rescue"). That is surely a reason for the people of Israel to sing a *new* song, as the psalmist exhorts them to do!

As well as this historic context, the psalm is also clearly a Messianic psalm, looking forward to the coming reign of Christ (verse 9b: "He comes to judge the earth; He will judge the world in righteousness, and the peoples with equity"), and as such it is the psalm that Isaac Watts based his lovely Christmas carol "Joy to the World" on:

Joy to the World; the Lord is come!
Let earth receive her King!
Let ev'ry heart prepare Him room,
And heaven and nature sing.

This is a delightfully straightforward psalm; there are no caveats, no doubts at all in it, and it is from start to finish solely concerned with singing to the Lord and praising Him.

Sometimes it is good not to overanalyse our faith, and just rejoice in God's goodness!

Saturday, 20 June 2020

A quiet day at home. The garden is in peak growing season, and the combination of more rain and warm sun most days is causing a great sprouting of all our vegetables. They are coming along very well – as are the roses, and I spend another hour and a half pruning and dead-heading them.

The outside world continues to return to normality, with the pandemic slipping further down the news bulletins. Today is the first Saturday of the resumed football season too, and for the first time for three months the Saturday paper has a full sports section. My team lose to the bottom side in the league – some things don't change!

Psalm 99:
God is holy

Good morning. For the third time in the last few days, our psalm starts with the declaration "The Lord reigns". We are still in the sequence of Enthronement psalms, and today the psalmist concentrates on three aspects of God's reign; two we have met before and one new one.

The psalm is in three stanzas. In the first (verses 1-3), the psalmist describes God's greatness, and calls on the nations of earth to tremble before Him and exalt and praise His name. The psalmist then moves on (verses 4-5) to praise God's justice and fairness, and again calls on his listeners to exalt the Lord.

Both of these are familiar themes from the other Enthronement psalms we have been studying over the last few days. But the psalmist then introduces a third theme (verses 6-9), that of the God who answers. He answers both His priests (verse 6: "Moses, Aaron … Samuel, they called on the Lord, and He answered them") and the general people.

This willingness of God to listen to His people and to respond meets a great human need. We all know how frustrating it is when someone stays silent, ignores our emails, refuses to take our phone calls. For the Israelites, it was vital that God heard their cries *and responded*; indeed it was one of the contrasts with other gods that he did so. Recall the battle between Elijah and the 450 priests of Baal, where the priests called on Baal *and he did not answer* (1 Kings 18:26).

And yet, although He does indeed hear our prayers, we should not fall into the trap of overfamiliarity with God. Three times, once at the end of each stanza, the psalmist reminds us that God is holy. This combination of God's holiness, or separateness, yet willingness to listen to us was central to Israel's faith; it is even more central for us through Christ, "the Word made flesh and living among us".

Sunday, 21 June 2020

The summer solstice, though overcast skies mean that the evening is not as light for as long as some recently.

The virus seems to be going round the world from East to West: it started in China, then Europe was its epicentre, and now, while we in Europe seem to be emerging from the worst of it, the Americas (USA and Brazil especially) are suffering the worst. And there is news that it has reappeared in Beijing, too.

Psalm 100:
A universal summons to praise and thank God

Good morning. Although not usually considered an Enthronement psalm itself, today's psalm acts as a logical conclusion to the little sequence we have been studying for the past week or so. After focusing on God's reign, we are now enjoined to respond with exuberant praise and thanksgiving.

The psalm combines clear instructions on *how* to praise God, full of commands and exhortations, with two verses explaining *why* we should do so. The people are to praise and thank the Lord both for what He is – "the Lord is God" (verse 2), "the Lord is Good" (verse 5); and for what He has done – "it is He who made us, and we are His" (verse 3).

The psalm was probably written to be used by a procession approaching and entering the temple, and the church has long used it to summon the faithful to worship. Its most familiar setting for us is the hymn by William Kethe, a 16th century Scotsman, the first verse of which is:

All people that on earth do dwell,
Sing to the Lord with cheerful voice.
Him serve with fear, His praise forth tell;
Come ye before Him and rejoice.

This hymn, with the accompanying melody "Old One Hundredth" as arranged by Vaughan Williams, was sung as the processional hymn for the coronation service of Queen Elizabeth II at Westminster Abbey in 1953. It is clearly a favourite of the Queen's; she also asked for it to be sung at the services celebrating both her Golden Jubilee in 2002 and her Diamond Jubilee ten years later.

It's not hard to see why this might be so. There is not a downbeat note or hint of hesitation in the whole of the psalm: God is praised from start to finish, and the whole earth and all its peoples are called to worship Him. What a wonderful joyous psalm!

Monday, 22 June 2020

The weather looks to be set for a mini-heatwave; the grey skies of recent days have gone and it is certainly warming up nicely. Let us hope the good weather lasts until the weekend, when our daughter comes to stay.

Psalm 101:
Blueprint for a righteous reign, a blameless life

Good morning. Today we have a psalm of David, thought to have been composed early in his reign, in which he sets out how he intends to conduct both his personal life and his rule over Israel. The ideal that David sets himself includes three main components: to sing to the Lord and praise Him (verse 1), to lead a blameless life (verses 2-4), and to govern fairly and hold his ministers and advisers to the same high standards (verses 4-8).

These are high ideals indeed, and David also knew that, without God's help, he would not be able to fulfil them. Hence in verse 2, he says "I will be careful to lead a blameless life – when will You come to me?", here calling on God to be with him and help him in his endeavours. David wanted his reign and his life to be inspired by God, led by God, enabled by God.

Nor was this commitment to God and a blameless life merely for public show. David pledges to walk uprightly with God even in his own house (verse 2b), where no-one except God can see him. And his declared aim is certainly ambitious and uncompromising: "I will have nothing to do with evil" (verse 4b). No half measures there.

Even with God's help and guidance, David would fall short, as all earthly kings do, as indeed everyone does. But that does not negate the desire to lead a righteous life – we should never let the fact that we will inevitably fall short of the perfect stop us from aiming to live our lives as close to God's ideal as we can.

Many kings throughout history have at least started their reign inspired by David's psalm setting out the path of righteous kingship. We may not be kings in control of others, but we are in control of our own conduct, and it should be a guide for us too.

Tuesday, 23 June 2020

Three months to the day after announcing the start of the lockdown, the government announces a major easing of the restrictions from 4 July, with restaurants, pubs, barbers and much else soon allowed to open, and the two-metre social distancing rule relaxed a bit. There are still some restrictions though – the rules are relaxed not abolished completely – and it will be interesting to see what dining and drinking out looks like after what is inevitably being called "Independence Day".

Psalm 102:
Pouring out one's woes to God

Good morning. Our psalm today is titled "A prayer of an afflicted man", and it is counted among the Penitential psalms, of which we have seen several already, most notably perhaps Psalm 38. It follows the usual format of the psalmist laying out his woes in front of God, drawing strength from God's promise to remember His faithful, and ending with reassurance and praise. Unlike most other Penitential psalms, though, there is less sign of remorse or repentance; it seems that the psalmist is so in despair that all he can do is call on the Lord for mercy.

The psalmist opens with a call to God to hear him (verses 1-2), and then describes his distress. He is both physically afflicted, taunted by his enemies and, worst of all, he feels under the wrath of God (verse 10).

These are deeply personal troubles, and it is thus something of a surprise when the psalm changes tone at verse 12 and the psalmist recalls God's promise not to the individual believer but to Zion. We move from individual sorrow and suffering to national salvation and restoration, as verses 12-22 offer a call to remember God's unchanging and everlasting sovereignty and unending care for His people, and a vision of a restored Zion responding with worship to God.

In the closing part of the psalm (verses 23-28), the psalmist has not forgotten his personal woes completely – he asks for longer life in verse 24 – but he seems calmed, even uplifted, by considering the future generations who will know and praise the Lord. And so, after praying this prayer, the psalmist ends at peace, not so much from relief of his physical suffering, but from the greater joy of a closer knowledge of God.

Wednesday, 24 June 2020

A frustrating day on the IT front as, firstly, we are without wi-fi, and then a migration of my website also goes wrong. The wi-fi problem is potentially serious – we have all learnt how dependent we are on broadband at home – and as soon as I had spotted it late on Tuesday and told my ISP, they responded very quickly by sending a replacement router by post. Alas, Royal Mail fail on their side of the bargain and, despite coming by urgent express delivery, it does not arrive today as promised.

As for my website, there is confusion over where and by whom it is hosted, and it seems that the various location pointers connecting its name to its IP address no longer sync. One for the pros to sort out – well beyond me! I shall go to my "AA" IT man – as in: "I can't do it but I know a man who can" (a phrase from an AA advert from the late 1980s!).

Psalm 103: Praise the Lord O my soul

Good morning. Our psalm today is a psalm of praise, one of the greatest calls to praise God in the whole Book of Psalms. It is attributed to David and, although there is no indication of when in his life he composed it, it reads like the psalm of someone later in life who has seen a lifetime of God's blessings and can reflect fully on them.

David starts by reminding himself of his personal reasons to praise God; in verses 3-5 the word "you" is singular, as he lists a number of ways in which God has intervened in his life: to forgive his sins, to heal his diseases, to redeem him when he was in danger, and so on. He then broadens this out (verses 6-18) into a longer recital of God's character and actions on behalf of the people of Israel, and all the faithful, and following this he repeats the call to praise the Lord, widening it to all creation, both on earth and in heaven (verses 19-22). And finally (verse 23) he narrows it right back down to the personal, and closes with the simple self-command "Praise the Lord, O my soul".

There is so much to enjoy in this hymn of praise. It concentrates entirely on God; there are no prayers for the psalmist's current situation or needs, there are no doubts, there are no promises for future faithfulness or worship – nothing to distract the psalmist from praising him now. And, as such, the psalm can be used by anyone at any time of their life, whether in sickness or health, calmness or stressful difficulties, sorrow or joy. Truly, a psalm for all seasons.

Thursday, 25 June 2020

A tense day on the IT side as, with the help of the pros at my ISP, I sort out my twin issues of the last two days, and fortunately with complete success! Our new router is safely installed and beaming wi-fi round the house, and all is well with my website too. Much relief all round.

It is very hot today; the hottest day of the year so far. The temperature in the conservatory, a complete sun-trap under glass, tops 50°C – far too hot to sit in it. More worryingly, the combination of announced relaxations in the lockdown from next month plus the very hot weather has people flocking to the public parks and beaches as if the pandemic was over. Great crowds and no way that social distancing can be maintained. But all the evidence from other countries ahead of us in the evolution of the pandemic shows that it is not over, that the risks of a second wave are still there, and there is a growing fear that we are storing up more trouble for later next month.

Psalm 104:
Sing praises to God the Creator

Good morning. If yesterday's psalm was a great hymn of praise to God the Redeemer, today's rivals it as a similar hymn of praise to God the Creator. It is not the only psalm to laud God through His creation – Psalm 8, which we met early in our travels through the Book of Psalms, is on the same theme – but it is perhaps the most magnificent recitation of all God's works in the Psalter, if not the whole of the Bible.

The psalmist is keen not to leave anything out, and for the first two-thirds of the psalm he quite closely follows the creation story in Genesis 1. Starting with the heavens and the form of the earth, he lists the introduction of dry land (verses 7 9), vegetation (verses 14-16), living creatures (verses 17-18 and 21-22) and finally man (verse 23).

The psalmist next sings of how all living creatures depend on God not only for their existence but also for their for their well-being (verses 24-30), before concluding that the only proper response is to praise the Lord (verse 33: "I will sing to the Lord all my life; I will sing praise to my God as long as I live").

After a brief aside on the fate of the wicked in verse 35 – which somewhat breaks the flow and seems if anything a little out of place in such a glorious song of praise – the psalmist closes today's psalm in the same way that yesterday's ended, with the simple command "Praise the Lord, O my soul. Praise the Lord".

Friday, 26 June 2020

Our elder daughter makes use of the relaxations in the lockdown to come to stay with us for a few days today. It is good to see her – video calls apart (and they are good, but not the same), we have not seen her for three months except briefly at Vicky's mother's funeral. Both she and Vicky are both excellent cooks and enjoy cooking together, so we are in for some fine dining over the next few days!

In the afternoon we visit Denbies, a large winery in the Surrey Hills which is open to visit, walk around the vineyards and shop at their winery shop. Which we do to great effect – their sparkling wine is extremely good and we both take the opportunity to lay in some supplies.

The extremely hot weather has one last hurrah in the afternoon but then breaks; as the front passes over it goes grey, much cooler (perhaps falling 15° in as many minutes) and even turns a little wet. Much needed relief, for both the garden and us alike!

Psalm 105:
God the Sovereign Actor in Israel's history

Good morning. Our psalm today is one of the small number of "History psalms", similar to Psalm 78. Their intention was to remind the people of Israel of their history and of God's repeated actions on their behalf. The first 15 verses of the psalm are also found in 1 Chronicles 16, where David sings them to celebrate the bringing of the Ark to Jerusalem, though it is not clear whether David himself composed the psalm for the occasion or was merely reciting a well-known existing song.

The psalm opens with a general summons to praise the Lord (verses 1-4), and then a specific command to remember His works (verses 5-6: "Remember the wonders He has done, His miracles, and the judgments He pronounced, O descendants of Abraham His servant, O sons of Jacob, His chosen ones"). The remainder of the psalm recounts the times that God has intervened in Israel's history, starting from Abraham and running through to their deliverance from Egypt and time in the Wilderness. The psalm closes with a summary (verse 42: "He remembered His holy promise given to His servant Abraham"), and the psalmist's conclusion (verses 44-45: "He gave them the lands of the nations … that they might keep His precepts and observe His laws").

In this and the two preceding psalms we have seen three aspects of God, and been given three appropriate responses. In Psalm 103, the psalmist sang of God the Loving Redeemer, to whom the appropriate response is praise. In Psalm 104, the psalmist details God the All-powerful Creator, to whom the appropriate response is awe and worship. Today, we read of God the Sovereign Actor in Israel's history, faithful to His covenant promise, to whom the appropriate response is observation of His laws. We will see in tomorrow's psalm how well the people of Israel kept to this command.

Saturday, 27 June 2020

A quieter (and thankfully cooler) day at home; much cooking in the afternoon and we enjoy a fine dinner drawing on Greek, Turkish and even Persian influences. Quite delicious.

The country feels tense ahead of next weekend's partial relaxation to the lockdown. Will people obey social distancing? The evidence of a few sunny days and the resulting overcrowded beaches and social problems is not encouraging. Then again, will anyone actually want to go to a restaurant with all the restrictions?

Psalm 106:
Israel's repeated disobedience

Good morning. After three psalms describing different aspects of God's nature and faithfulness to Israel and His Covenant, today's psalm details Israel's response. It is in essence another History psalm, the counterpart to Psalm 105, but its tone is more that of a national lament, even confession. If the overarching theme of Psalm 105 was "Remember God and His works", then the theme of today's psalm is "But Israel forgot His works and ignored God".

The psalmist starts with a call to praise the Lord, and prays that he may be included among God's people and share in their salvation (verses 1-5). The main part of the psalm (verses 6-43) details the many instances since the Exodus where Israel had fallen short. This is not just a historical account: the psalmist does not spare his own generation, as the list of Israel's failings is preceded by the confession (verse 6) "We have sinned even as our fathers did; we have done wrong and acted wickedly". This is a direct and unequivocal statement: the psalmist wants his audience to be in no doubt that they too are part of the national history of disobeying God, that they too need His forgiveness.

Having established that Israel's past is characterised by disobedience to God, and that Israel's present is no different, the psalmist changes to supplication, recalling God's past mercy to their forefathers (verses 44-46) and asking that He would once again come to their aid and that they too might be saved (verse 47). And he then closes both the psalm and Book IV of the Psalms with a doxology of praise.

The message of Psalms 105 and 106, taken together, is the unchanging nature of God and the unchanging weakness of man. And I reflect on our own generation: we are no different from the generation the psalmist first spoke to – we are weak and disobedient like them and, like them, we need God's salvation.

Sunday, 28 June 2020

With our daughter staying with us we plan a barbecue in the garden, and her boyfriend is able to visit for the day too – properly socially distancing, as he is only in the garden (and can get to it going round, not through, the house). Elaborate precautions, but good to see him again. Alas the weather does not really co-operate, and on two separate occasions there is a complete cloudburst and part of the party has to shelter in the garage! But the sun is hot and the patio dried up fast enough, and the barbecue was excellent.

Psalm 107:
God's care of His people through the ages

Good morning. Although today's psalm is the opening psalm of Book V of the Psalter, it has much in common with the psalms immediately before it at the end of Book IV. It is a recitation of the many ways in which God helps His faithful people when they face difficulties or adversities, punctuated by calls to the people to learn and give thanks to the Lord.

After an opening general exhortation to give thanks, the main body of the psalm gives four separate instances of God's loving care. The psalmist details how God guides and sustains those who are lost (verses 4-7), disciplines and then delivers sinners (verses 10-14), rescues the disobedient and brings them back to His Word (verses 17-20) and saves those facing storms at sea (verses 23-30). Each of these four mini-sermons on God's response to the difficulties His people find themselves in is ended with the refrain "Let them give thanks to the Lord for His unfailing love, and His wonderful deeds for men".

The last part of the psalm is seen by some commentators as referring again to Israel's history, though the allusions are somewhat vague. As opposed to the earlier part of the psalm, here the psalmist is making contrasts: God turns rivers into deserts for the wicked, but restores the land's fruitfulness for the faithful (verses 33-38); He humbles the proud, but lifts up the needy and the upright (verses 39-42).

After this magnificent exposition on how God acts in the world of men and cares for His people, the psalmist ends with a simple verse: "Whoever is wise, let him heed these things and consider the great love of the Lord". Am I wise? Do I consider the love of the Lord? How should I respond?

Monday, 29 June 2020

Our daughter returns to her home after a most enjoyable long weekend with us – we will be eating more frugally for the next few days as we recover from the gastronomic extravaganza!

The fears of a re-emergence of the virus are heightened by an outbreak in Leicester, which is sufficiently severe for the government to reimpose a fairly full local lockdown. How this will be enforced without roadblocks is not exactly clear.

Psalm 108:
Confidence in God's victories

Good morning. After the longer and more analytical psalms of recent days we are back with King David as our psalmist today and, as tends to be his style, he gives us a shorter psalm, a more direct hymn of praise.

Today's psalm is unusual in that it is composed from parts of two earlier psalms: verses 1-5 replicate Psalm 57 (verses 7-11), and verses 6-13 are a copy of Psalm 60 (verses 5-12). In both cases David has taken the most positive part of his earlier psalms. Psalm 57 is, in the main, a personal lament, and Psalm 60 more of a collective lament on behalf of the people of Israel, but for this psalm David has chosen just the most upbeat and God-focused parts of them.

David was not short of ways to sing about the Lord, and will have had a purpose in deciding to re-use his earlier writings like this. To me that purpose is clear: the result of David's editing is that all of the doubts in the earlier psalms have been excised, and we are left instead with a strong statement of personal praise of God (verses 1-5) and collective confidence in His victories (verses 6-13). From the opening declaration of praise to the closing prayer, the watchwords of this psalm are steadfastness, triumph, victory, and faith is clearly at work throughout the psalm.

I find this an uplifting psalm from a man who knew troubled times in his life but never lost his faith and trust in the Lord, and never doubted God's final victory.

Tuesday, 30 June 2020

I am relieved to see that my latest Laburnum Consulting article, on the economic costs and consequences of the lockdown, is well received; it is challenging to write on the financial side of the pandemic and the lockdown against the background of the human implications of thousands of lives lost, and I was quite nervous that some people might take it the wrong way and think it insensitive. But fortunately most of my readers appear to have understood the rationale for the article and even agreed with it.

A bit of a blow for Vicky as she looks to order wool for her next major knitting project, only to find that there is none to be had. All the suppliers of the particular wool she wants are completely sold out. So alongside turning to growing vegetables and home-baking, the nation has apparently also taken up knitting during the lockdown!

Psalm 109: Calling for God's vengeance on the wicked

Good morning. We come today to one of the most challenging of the psalms, a psalm that has divided Christians throughout history. It is an Imprecatory psalm, in which David is calling on God for vengeance against his enemies. The litany of curses that David delivers in verses 6-20 is violent and probably the strongest in the whole of the Old Testament; they sit oddly with David's known merciful nature when he was king and challenge us directly when we consider Christ's teaching that we should love our enemies and turn the other cheek. Some authorities have even called for the psalm to be omitted from the Church's canon and order of regular worship; while that might be an extreme reaction, it is hard to see a modern Christian congregation singing the psalm with enjoyment.

Nevertheless, the compilers of the Book of Psalms thought it worthy of inclusion, and we should therefore study it as God's revealed word. And there are several points that I take from it.

Firstly, David opens in prayer and sets out before God his innocence (verses 1-5). This I think is fundamental: only the innocent can pray as David does here. Secondly, for all the fire and brimstone in the verses of imprecation, David at all times leaves the matter to God and does not take things into his own hands – even, as we have observed, when he was later in a position to do so. Thirdly, having poured out his desire for God's vengeance, David turns in the last third of the psalm to a prayer for God's mercy and protection, before finally (verses 30-31) ending as he so often does with a declaration of praise.

There is one other thought that underpins the whole of the psalm, and this is that there is indeed a price to pay for sin; God will indeed sit in judgment, and the wicked will indeed suffer His wrath. David is not in the end asking for anything outside either the Jewish understanding of God's righteous nature, or ours. It is sometimes tempting to airbrush this out of our faith, and focus entirely on God the loving merciful Father, but we should never forget the Day of Judgment, and the awful nature of God's wrath, and this psalm helps to remind me of this.

Wednesday, 1 July 2020

The news on the virus from around the world continues to be concerning, with the disease largely out of control in parts of America – the USA is experiencing over 50,000 new infections every day, and Brazil is not far behind. And even in countries that had largely controlled it, such as Australia, there are renewed outbreaks, and parts of Melbourne are back in full lockdown. In the UK, the local lockdown in Leicester is not going well: it is difficult to police public acceptance of it and adherence to the rules is notably less complete than it was when the nationwide lockdown was introduced at the end of March.

The very dry spring has had me using our watering systems much more than usual, and various of the hoses are worn out. A major leak in the main one that I use for the back garden – well, it is probably 20 years old! – makes me bite the bullet, and I spend the day repairing some and replacing or renewing others.

Psalm 110:
God the Father speaks to Christ the Messiah

Good morning. Today's short psalm is from start to finish messianic, and overtly looks forward to Jesus and His reign. It is quoted frequently in the New Testament, most notably by Jesus Himself, who challenged the religious leaders to interpret it (see for example Mark 12:35-37), but also by Peter at the first Pentecost (Acts 2:34-35), by Paul and several times by the writer of Hebrews.

The format of the psalm is unique: it is written by David, who appears to have been allowed to overhear a private conversation between God and His Son. The opening line "The Lord says to my Lord" contains three separate persons: in the original Hebrew, "The Lord" is *Yahweh* or God, "my Lord" is *Adonai* or Master, and the "my" refers to David, the psalmist.

In these seven short verses, God declares to His Son that he will be both Sovereign King (verses 1-3), eternal High Priest (verse 4), and Conqueror, victorious over all his enemies (verses 5-7). He also explains the conundrum that Jesus is "David's son" but nevertheless greater by far than David, Israel's greatest earthly king who, while an absolute ruler, was never also the high priest. The language is straightforward, and God's intentions are crystal clear.

What an extraordinary image this psalm gives us! What a revelation into God's divine purpose! What a privilege to read and marvel at these words! I am left once again to reflect on how God has so repeatedly communicated His plan to us through the Scriptures; there is no excuse for not understanding it, and the only question is to ask myself how I respond.

Thursday, 2 July 2020

International news is to the fore this morning as China has, as expected, imposed its new security law on Hong Kong. It is breath-taking in its scope and severity: a very wide description of what constitutes dissent and subversion, secret trials, extradition to the Mainland, no appeals, global reach (China claims the right to arrest and detain anyone, anywhere in the world, of any nationality, who writes or says anything they disapprove of).

The global reach they will not be able to enforce – though it will make its critics more nervous about visiting Hong Kong or China itself – but for the people of Hong Kong, it represents a complete crushing of their political freedoms and the end of the "One country, two systems" regime they were promised until 2047.

The West is predictably vocal in its disapproval, but, in truth, countries like Germany need China's trade and will do little concrete to upset them, while countries like America and Australia, China has long since decided to ignore. The UK has responded by offering Hong Kong's BNO ("British National Overseas") passport holders residence rights and a route to British citizenship; this is a brave and principled move that will infuriate China (and further put our relationship with them in the deep freeze), but for the moment it has widespread support on both sides of the political divide and across the country.

A sad day for Hong Kong as the flame of freedom is totally extinguished; an ominous day for the world as China flexes its muscles and shows ever more clearly both its aggressive nature and its total lack of concern for international treaties, norms or opinion.

Psalm 111:
Sing praises for God's works

Good morning. There is much to enjoy in today's psalm, for all its brevity, and beyond the surface level of praise for God's works I have found it worth re reading for its deeper thoughts. It is also one of the Acrostic psalms; after the opening line "Praise the Lord", each of the 22 lines starts with a successive letter of the Hebrew alphabet.

Verse 1 starts with an exhortation – "Praise the Lord" – but also, a commitment by the psalmist to follow his own advice. How often we forget this, but if we want others to follow our advice and turn to the Lord, we must be seen to do so ourselves!

The main body of the psalm is an enumeration of the many ways in which God has provided for His people. The psalm differs from the Historical psalms, which list actual events in Israel's history, and instead generalises to God's ongoing care for the faithful: we are not meant here to be reminded of specific instances, but instead to reflect on the constant all-enveloping care that God shows us. The psalmist explicitly directs us to do this in verse 2: "Great are the works of the Lord; they are pondered by all who delight in them".

The psalm ends with a single verse that stands slightly apart, but which contains one of the great statements of the Bible: "The fear of the Lord is the beginning of wisdom". I find it necessary to re-interpret both the word "fear" and the word "wisdom" here; neither really have their modern 21st century meaning of "terror" and "knowledge" respectively. Rather, the psalmist is saying that a reverence for the Lord makes a person receptive to God's wisdom, opens the way for a deeper understanding of God.

But for me, I return to verse 2b as the key to this psalm, and will ponder afresh the works of the Lord.

Friday, 3 July 2020

At last Vicky's father is allowed home from hospital, after three weeks and several false starts. Vicky takes him home, and will be taking close care of him as he gets back on his feet. It has been a long haul for him.

Psalm 112:
God's blessings for the righteous

Good morning. Today's psalm is the pair to yesterday's; like Psalm 111 it is an Acrostic psalm with 10 verses, and the structure of the psalm is also identical: an opening call to praise, the body of the psalm on a single theme and then a closing verse of slight contrast. There are also strong similarities in the wording of individual verses. The two are clearly meant to be taken together therefore; the first is a psalm about God and His works, while the second is a psalm about the godly man and his response.

Verse 1b, "Blessed is the man who fears the Lord, who finds delight in His commands", sets the tone for the psalm. Again we must read "fear" as "revere", and this verse tells us that we must revere and worship the Lord by obeying Him. And if we do, the psalmist says, God's blessings will flow to us, and much of the rest of the psalm describes these blessings in glowing detail.

Although much of the psalm is about the blessings that the godly will receive, the psalmist has included a pair of examples of what the godly will themselves do in response, as in verse 5 we read that the God-fearing believer will be "generous and lend freely", and will "conduct his affairs with justice". His generosity is noted again in verse 9: "He has scattered abroad his gifts to the poor".

As in yesterday's psalm, there is a change of tone with the last verse, and we see how the wicked will observe the good fortune of the faithful as they receive God's blessings, and will despair – though they will not, apparently, change their minds and repent!

For me, I pick out one verse from the two psalms to reflect more on: verse 3b, which in each psalm reads identically. "His righteousness endures for ever", declares the psalmist, in Psalm 111 referring to God, in Psalm 112 to the godly. God and man together, for ever. Hallelujah!

Saturday, 4 July 2020

The day the lockdown is relaxed and, although there are many separate relaxations, the one that all the papers highlight is "The pubs are open!". The Chancellor urges people to "go out and spend" – the big fear is that people will still be too nervous to so do, but on the whole people do appear to be happy to go out, and although there are inevitably stories of drunken revelling, most crowds are well behaved and distanced.

Psalm 113:
Praise for the supreme God who cares for His people

Good morning. As we are discovering, Book V of the Book of Psalms, which started with Psalm 107, is full of psalms of praise, and today we start a set of six psalms (Psalms 113-118) that are collectively known as "the Egyptian Hallel". *Hallel* is the Hebrew for praise (it is the first part of the word Hallelujah), and these six psalms are in Jewish tradition sung at great feasts, especially the Passover feast. It is very likely that when Jesus and His disciples "sang a hymn" after the Last Supper (Matthew 26:30), it would have been one of the psalms in this set.

In today's psalm, the psalmist picks out two characteristics of God for us to direct our praise towards. After an opening call to praise the Lord "both now and for evermore", verses 3-5 extol the majesty of God, enthroned on high, far above the heavens, over all the nations. But then suddenly the psalm pivots at verse 6, and this Supreme Deity "stoops down to look on … the earth". And in verses 7-9, the psalmist sings of His care for the poor, the needy, the unhappy.

We are used to the high and mighty keeping themselves separate from us, the masses. The gates at the entrance to Downing Street, the elaborate protocol around the Royal Family – this is the normal state of affairs. Which is what makes God's involvement with and care for His people so remarkable, and so worthy of great praise, as the psalmist reminds us.

For us as Christians, the culmination of this care for us, this involvement in our human world, was that He came to earth Himself, in the form of Jesus, His Son. We are all so familiar with this that it is easy to lose sight of quite how extraordinary an event this is, and I shall use this psalm, and its dramatic pivot at verse 6, to praise afresh the God who came to be our Emmanuel, or "God with us".

Sunday, 5 July 2020

A sunny day, but very windy. The pubs continue to do good business, especially those with gardens, but we are not tempted to join the crowds – Vicky finds and clearly enjoys a most apposite quote from Samuel Pepys' diary in 1665 that "a dram in exchange for the pox is an ill bargain indeed". More seriously, since she remains the main provider of much of her father's needs, we do have to remain more careful than most.

It is also the 72nd anniversary of the creation of the NHS in 1948. I don't recall it ever been marked before or even commented on, but this year it features prominently in the news – the "NHS's birthday", as the tabloid press inevitably call it.

Psalm 114: A poetic recalling of the Exodus

Good morning. Today's short psalm is a hymn recalling the Exodus. It stands well enough on its own, but would normally have been sung by the Israelites alongside yesterday's psalm as the two introductions to the Passover feast.

The language of the psalm is highly poetic, and for the first six verses the psalmist almost playfully hides God's power and authority over events. In verse 1, "When Israel came out of Egypt", God's hand in their escape is not mentioned – it is as if it was the people's own actions that gave them their freedom. In verse 2, the psalmist presents God as finding a home in the Promised Land, as if He was the lost and wandering one, not His people. In verses 3-6, again the emphasis is on the actions of others – in this case the sea, the mountains, the earth itself – and the presence of God as the cause of all these happenings is implied but not made explicit.

It is not until the last two verses that the psalmist turns to the Lord, and directs the earth (and by implication all who dwell on it) to tremble in His presence. And the last verse is, for me, a lovely link back to yesterday's psalm; just as Psalm 113 ended with God making the barren woman full of life and children, so today's psalm ends with God making the barren rocks full of life and water. A picture of "the Lord, the giver of life" – as we say in the Nicene creed.

A psalm to read and enjoy; and I am left grateful that when the compilers of the Books of Psalms decided which to include, alongside all the meatier and more serious psalms of repentance, reverence and praise, they also found room for beautiful little poems like today's psalm.

Monday, 6 July 2020

My phone is full of pictures of people "before and after" their first trip to the barber for four months – a social historian in 100 years' time will conclude that what we all worried about most in the lockdown was the length and tidiness of our hair!

That and the pubs, of course. But already there are reports of pubs closing again, after people who visited them at the weekend have tested positive for the virus. Not many as yet, but I hope not a harbinger of things to come.

Psalm 115:
God in His heaven, caring for the world

Good morning. Today's psalm is a congregational hymn, a call to focus on the Lord and trust in Him. It is a strong statement of confidence in the Lord's provision for His people. In form, it is written as a "verse and response" duet between the people and a leader: the people open by singing verses 1-8, the leader comes in with verses 9-11, the people respond with verses 12-13, the leader comes in a second time with verses 14-15, and the people then close the singing with verses 16-18.

The psalmist opens with a call for God's name to be glorified, and then (verses 2-8) contrasts God with the gods and idols of other nations. There is much unspoken here in the attack on the idols of other nations, an implied contrast between the visible but impotent gods and idols of the heathen, made by man, and the invisible but all-powerful God of Israel, not made by man but the Maker of man.

The first call by the leader (verses 9-11) is to trust the Lord; the call is made to three groups of people: "O house of Israel" (i.e., the Israelite nation), "O house of Aaron" (i.e., the priests) and "Ye who fear Him" (i.e., the faithful, here not limited to Israel but across the nations). After the people duly respond that they are blessed, the second call by the leader (verses 14-15) pronounces and confirms the blessing on the people, and the people's second respond is praise.

I have a great sense of God and His people at one here, a confidence in God's rule and a gratefulness for His care. As the poet Browning wrote, "God's in His heaven, all's right with the world".

Tuesday, 7 July 2020

We decide it is time to make a start on some of the many jobs that have arisen over the last few months that require a handyman, and I contact first of all a plumber and an electrician. The electrician replies immediately; he is back at work and, provided I can find the light fittings I want, he will be able to come round. I go to the shop and there is no queue and the fittings are in stock, so we can proceed. Life is getting closer to normal!

Psalm 116:
Gratitude for rescue from death

Good morning. We have a psalm of thanksgiving today, and one of an intensely personal nature as the psalmist declares his gratitude to the Lord for saving him – note the repeated use of the words *I* and *my* throughout the psalm.

Unusually, the psalmist starts with a declaration of *love* for the Lord. More commonly, psalms speak of praise for the Lord or trust in Him, but here the psalmist sets the more personal and emotional tone of the psalm right at the start, as love carries more the sense of devotion and personal loyalty to God.

In the next section, verses 3-11, the psalmist describes how he was rescued by God. He called on God, was heard, and was saved. There is no sense here that the psalmist's love is transactional, as in "You save me, and I will love You"; there was no bargaining with God before God acted, and it is a pure and natural response to mercies received. And in the rest of the psalm, the psalmist first asks (verse 12) and then answers (verses 13-19) how he will show his love and gratitude. Importantly, the psalmist vows four times to give his thanks and praise to God in public (verses 14, 18 and 19 twice), so that all may see and hear it and learn of the works of the Lord.

Although the psalm appears to be about rescue from physical death, it is equally applicable to those facing spiritual death through sin. And so all who accept Christ as Saviour can say with the psalmist the words of verses 8 and 9: "You, O Lord, have delivered me from death … that I may walk before the Lord in the land of the living". My challenge is then to also join the psalmist in the rest of the psalm too, to "love the Lord" and "fulfil my vows to Him in the presence of all his people".

Wednesday, 8 July 2020

Another sign of returning normality: cricket returns, with the start of the First Test versus the West Indies. No crowds allowed at the game (county cricketers will be used to that!) but that other ever-present at English test matches – the rain – makes a full appearance and curtails the day's play. Where would we be without that well-known phrase of the English summer: "And now over to the Test Match, where rain has stopped play"?

A much colder and wetter day all round in fact, and for the first time for many days a long-trousers-and-jersey day. After the glorious weather of spring, it seems that Mother Nature is also returning more to normality!

Psalm 117:
A call to all nations to praise the Lord

Good morning. Psalm 117 is well known as the shortest psalm and, at two verses, the shortest chapter in the whole Bible. It is also the middle chapter of the whole Bible: there are 1,189 chapters in the Old and New Testaments combined, and Psalm 117 is the 595th.

But despite its brevity, the psalm is complete in form and has one of the most powerful messages of any psalm. In form it has the common three-part construction, with a call to praise (verse 1), a reason for praise (verse 2a) and a command at the close (verse 2b). In content, the psalm is unusual in being addressed to all peoples; indeed in many translations the opening phrase is not "Praise the Lord, all you nations" but "Praise the Lord, all you *Gentiles*", and this makes this psalm the only psalm directly and specifically addressed to the non-Jewish peoples. And the message the Gentiles are given is that they too should praise God, not because He is powerful, but because of His great love and faithfulness. What a message!

We are so familiar with the idea of a universal God, a God for all people, that we perhaps fail to comprehend how unusual this would have been in the time of ancient Israel. Most peoples had their own gods, jealously kept to themselves, and the idea of "our god" being interested in, let alone worshipped by, foreigners was very alien. But right from the promise to Abraham, God made it clear that, although Israel was His chosen people, His promise was not limited to Israel, and their role was not to keep God exclusively to themselves but to proclaim Him to all peoples as the supreme God.

This psalm is not just a call to all peoples to praise the Lord; it is a reminder to Israel of their unique role in God's plan for the world. Since God does nothing by chance, I wonder if the fact that Psalm 117 is the central chapter of the Bible is meant to signify that it is also the central *message* of the Bible.

Thursday, 9 July 2020

The City Livery Club, like all the livery companies and so many other organisations besides, has had to suspend its calendar of events and has put in place some Zoom meetings instead. Today Vicky and I took part in a quiz on the City. Good fun, and nice to see familiar faces – we thought we had done quite respectably but were well behind the winners!

Psalm 118:
Giving thanks for the Lord's salvation

Good morning. The last of the set of six "Egyptian Hallel" psalms is a celebration and thanksgiving for the work of the Lord, and for His salvation for His people. It is intensely focused on the Lord; the word appears 27 times in just 29 verses, and the psalmist keeps his mind on God throughout the psalm, from the first verse, "Give thanks to the Lord, for He is good; His love endures for ever", until the last, where the same exhortation is repeated to book-end the psalm.

Much of the psalm (verses 5-21) is in the first person, and appears to be a leader relating his personal experience of God's mercy, ending with a concluding summary in verse 21: "I will give You thanks for You answered me; You have become my salvation". At this point the people take over and respond, rejoicing and praising God for His mercy to the psalmist and to His people in general.

There is so much to enjoy and give thanks for in this psalm, from the repeated praise for God's mercy and salvation to the call in verse 24: "This is the day the Lord has made; let us rejoice and be glad in it", a command that loses none of its force through being so familiar to us. The psalm also contains many messianic references and Jesus refers directly to Himself as "the stone the builders rejected" (verse 22), which becomes the capstone of God's church (see for example Matthew 21:42).

But for both power and simplicity, the verse I shall take and repeat through the day is verse 28: "You are my God, and I will give You thanks; You are my God, and I will exalt You".

Friday, 10 July 2020

The electrician comes and fits our new bathroom lights; he is neat, courteous and quick, and we can tick one more job off the "to do when the lockdown eases" list. And our cleaner returns; she is diplomatic about my attempts to keep the house clean in her four-month absence but clearly feels it needs her touch.

In the evening we hold at my instigation a Family Whisky Tasting by Zoom. Six whiskies, three from the Islands and three from Speyside, and it is deemed a great success. The organiser was knowledgeable and entertaining, and the choice of whiskies very good indeed. Even though I ordered half measures (2.5 cl of each whisky rather than the standard miniature bottle of 5 cl) it was still a good session, and Vicky and I followed it with haggis for dinner.

Psalm 119 (overview): The majesty of God's Word

Good morning. We arrive today at Psalm 119, the longest psalm in the Psalter by far and also the longest chapter in the whole Bible. It is far too long to do justice to in a single daily meditation, and today I will consider just its structure, before turning over the next few days to its content and detailed messages for us.

The psalm is an elaborate acrostic, with 22 stanzas of eight verses each; the stanzas are associated with the 22 letters of the Hebrew alphabet in sequence and, in each stanza, each verse starts with that letter. This is clearly a mnemonic, an aid for people to remember the verses as they studied and recited the psalm, and this gives us the insight that the psalm was meant for personal devotion as well as public prayer.

The overriding theme of the psalm is God's Word. The psalm uses at least eight difference terms for God's Word, including Law, Judgments, Testimonies, Commandments or Commands, Promises, Statutes, Precepts and two different Hebrew words both usually translated into English simply as Word. These are used in almost equal amounts, with none dominating, and almost every single verse of the psalm contains at least one of the terms.

This apart, there is no clear flow of thought in the psalm, no narrative. The stanzas are not obviously linked to each other; rather, the psalm is like a string of pearls, each one of value on its own but the whole necklace greater than the sum of its parts. Because of this, the psalm is often broken up and sung or studied in sections, as we will over the next few days.

But it is also worth reading the whole psalm through and allowing the greatness of God's Word to wash over you and overwhelm you. That is my preparation today for our study over the next few days!

Saturday, 11 July 2020

A most enjoyable day as we go to have lunch with our daughter in their still relatively new house. We saw it a couple of times before the lockdown, when they had just moved in, and they are very keen to show us all the work they have done on it since. They have used the lockdown well!

We return their pot plants and fish to them (he survives the journey, thank goodness), and they give us the most enormous and delicious meze lunch – elements of both Greek and Turkish cuisine. We roll back to New Malden very happy and not needing any dinner. A great joy to be able to see them again and a splendid day.

Psalm 119 (vv 1-48): The centrality of God's Word for the faithful

Good morning. We start our detailed study of Psalm 119 with a statement that in effect summarises the whole of the psalm, as verse 1 declares that "Blessed are they whose ways are blameless, who walk according to the law of the Lord". We might think of this as our spur to meditate on the psalm as we set out on our study of it: verse 1 sets the background, and then the rest of the psalm leads us deeper into understanding what it means! In fact, all of the first stanza urges us to hold to God's laws as we walk through life.

The second stanza (verses 9-16) encourages us not just to heed God's word but to internalise it ("hide it in my heart") so that it becomes not an external law we try to obey but an integral part of our life and very being. If we do this, the third stanza (verses 17-24) says, we will find the law a delight, we will long to hear God's word, we will (verse 24) be ever guided by it.

The fourth stanza (verses 25-32) introduces for the first time some setbacks and difficulties; the psalmist is laid low and weary. But he reiterates his steadfastness in holding to God's law, and in verse 32 introduces a new notion: by obeying God's law (and thus in one sense depriving himself of the liberty to do as he pleases), the psalmist declares that his heart has been set free.

In the fifth stanza (verses 33-40), the psalmist calls for the first time on God to help him. "Teach me to follow Your decrees", he says, "give me understanding". A desire to follow God's word is necessary but not sufficient; we also need help in understanding how to do so. And the sixth stanza (verses 41-48) serves as a summary of our first day studying this wonderful psalm, and I can say alongside the psalmist (verse 48): "I meditate on your decrees".

Sunday, 12 July 2020

A quiet Sunday at home. My replacement chimenea has arrived (the old one got too hot and cracked all over) and I give it its first gentle firing. Plans to use the old one as a planter come to naught though – I pick it up and it comes apart in my hands! The cracks from the overheating were clearly more serious than they looked and the decision to replace it is fully justified by events.

Vicky goes to her father for coffee; it is good that he is home, and that the restrictions have eased enough for her to enjoy sitting in the garden with him. A lovely sunny day for it too.

Psalm 119 (vv 49-96): Seeking a deeper understanding of God's Word

Good morning. We continue our study of Psalm 119 with a look at stanzas 7-12. They offer a continuation of the psalmist's meditation on God's word, reflecting in turn on how God's law and promises give hope and comfort (stanzas 7 and 11, verses 49-56 and 81-88), and how the psalmist replies by promising to obey God's commandments (stanza 8, verses 57-64) and by asking for more teaching so that he can do so more faithfully (stanza 9, verses 65-72) and have a deeper understanding of the laws (stanza 10, verses 73-80).

There is a sense in this sequence that real life is reasserting itself. The psalm's opening, which we looked at yesterday, was in many ways idyllic; there was no hint of the psalmist suffering any of life's misfortunes until the fourth stanza. But here, reality is all around the psalmist: the actions and scorn of the faithless, the challenge of really knowing and understanding God's word, even (verses 71 and 75) righteous correction by God. Throughout, the psalmist's response is to hold to God's commandments, to seek to know them better, to deepen his understanding, to come closer to God through His word.

And the reason for this is explained by the psalmist in the last stanza we look at today, stanza 12 (verses 89-96). Here he declares the eternal nature of God's word, a theme so fundamental that it is picked up at several places in the New Testament. Jesus Himself declares that "heaven and earth will pass away, but my words will never pass away" (Matthew 24:35), and Peter echoes this in his first epistle, saying that "The word of the Lord stands for ever" (1 Peter 1:25).

Half way through our study of the psalm, and we close today with verse 96b: "Your commands are boundless". For me, this points to the lesson from this meditation on God's word: the more I study it, the more I realise there is more to learn.

Monday, 13 July 2020

The council recycling and refuse centre is open again for general use, and I have four months' worth of rubbish to dispose of. It is "by pre-booked reservation only", which is novel – but the queues are just as long as before the pandemic when I get there! We also welcome our plumber, who is back working again, and he can finally address the leak in the bath (see 12 April). Frustratingly, he can't immediately find anything, but he tightens a few loose nuts and screws, and we hope this will do the trick.

Psalm 119 (vv 97-144): The love of God's Word

Good morning. The section of Psalm 119 we have for study this morning starts and ends with two statements that can stand as a summary of the whole psalm. We start with verse 97: "Oh, how I love Your law! I meditate on it all day long", and our chosen verses end with verse 144: "Your statutes are forever right; give me understanding that I may live".

What a complete picture we have in just these two verses of the psalmist's approach to God's word. Here we have both his boundless enthusiasm for the law, and his appreciation of its life-giving nature. But beyond that, we also have the key to the whole of his meditation in this psalm. Who would not love a gift from God that offered eternal life? And who, loving God's law, would not strive to obey it and follow its commandments? And who, seeking to obey God's statutes ever more closely, would not study them and try to understand them more deeply?

These themes run through all of the stanzas in today's study. In stanza 14 (verses 105-112) the law is likened to a lamp to guide the psalmist's feet, and he confirms his promise to follow the law, to accept teaching on it, to not forget it. They are, he says, "the joy of my heart" (verse 111). Later, he declares that he "stands in awe of Your laws" (stanza 15, verse 120), he repeatedly calls himself God's servant under the law (stanza 16, verses 122-125), and he describes God's word as "wonderful" (stanza 17, verse 129) and "righteous" (stanza 18, verses 137-138).

But one verse from this section gives me a more direct challenge, as in verse 136 the psalmist says "Streams of tears flow from my eyes, for Your law is not obeyed". The psalmist's devotion to God's law could not be more clear; does His word have the same place in my life?

Tuesday, 14 July 2020

Inevitably the new lights in the bathrooms have smaller fittings than the old ones, so there is some paint touch-up work to do on the ceiling. Not one of my regular skills but I give it a try and it looks OK.

Photography is also not something I am usually known for but some photos of sunsets over the sea that I submitted to a glossy magazine on Scottish Islands have, it seems, captured the editor's eye, and she gives me the great honour of a full-page spread, with stories attached to each photo. They have come out very pleasingly and even a photographer friend of mine is impressed!

Psalm 119 (vv 145-176): Coming closer to God through His Word

Good morning. For the fifth and last time we turn to Psalm 119, as we conclude our study of this great work of meditation on God's law. And today there is a change of tone, as the last four stanzas of the psalm see the psalmist turning from study of God's word to a greater realisation of how much he needs God Himself.

Thus the first stanza of today's study (stanza 19, verses 145-152) starts with the psalmist saying "I call with all my heart; answer me, O Lord", and continues in similar vein: "I call out to You; save me", "I rise before dawn and cry for help". And in stanza 20 he is more specific, asking for God's salvation – verses 153-160 are full of prayers to God to "deliver me", "redeem me", "preserve my life".

These prayers seem to have reassured the psalmist, as by stanza 21 he is again declaring (verses 165-166) that "Great peace have those who love Your law, and nothing can make them stumble. I wait for Your salvation, Lord, and I follow Your commands". And in the last stanza (verses 169-176) he offers a general prayer for long life and strength to praise the Lord. But finally, the psalm ends on a humbler note as, after all his meditation, the psalmist remembers his sinful tendencies and ends (verse 176) by asking God to "Seek Your servant, for I have not forgotten Your commands".

As we have journeyed with the psalmist through this long meditation on God's word – longer by number of verses than no less than 29 of the 66 books of the Bible – I have a growing sense of the true purpose of God's laws: they are not so much an end in themselves, a guide to righteous living for its own virtue (good though that is), as a way for the faithful believer to deepen their relationship with and come closer to God. That, for me, is the beauty of this magnificent psalm.

Wednesday, 15 July 2020

I am invited to join a discussion with the Chinese Ambassador today on the state of China-Europe relations. Quite a privilege, and very interesting. No real answers, of course, to why China is now pursuing a more aggressive and confrontational style, and indeed one did not expect any, but the complete double-speak of the seasoned diplomat is fascinating to observe. Everything is, naturally, everyone else's fault!

In the evening we have another family wine tasting by Zoom. A rather special Mâcon Lugny, and this time people have prepared elaborate food to go with it. First prize to Sam for homemade rillettes – we are all envious and ask for the recipe!

Psalm 120:
A prayer for deliverance from false accusers

Good morning. Our psalm this morning is entitled "A Song of Ascents"; it is the first of 15 consecutive psalms with this title, Psalms 120-134. There is some debate about what this title signifies; most scholars consider that the 15 psalms were to be sung by pilgrims travelling to Jerusalem and to the Temple for one of Israel's feast days, but it is by no means a settled view. They are however well established psalms of some antiquity, with four of the 15 attributed to David and one further to Solomon.

What is clear, though, in today's psalm is that the psalmist is a long way from Jerusalem and the house of the Lord, both literally and figuratively. He is living among non-believers and surrounded by lying and deceit, by people who live violent lives and have no desire for peace. And he cries out to the Lord for help.

Now, men have railed against an evil and unkind world and complained to random deities from the dawn of time, and of course still do so today. But the psalmist adds a small comment at the end of his opening verse that changes this from just another complaint into a profound statement about the God he worships, the one true God. The psalmist adds (verse 1b) "and He answers me" (or in some translations "and He hears me"), and it is this confidence that the Lord will hear his prayer, and will act to save him, that sustains the psalmist in his troubles and distress.

That we can address our prayers directly to the Almighty is a privilege in itself. That we can be confident that He will both hear us and respond to our needs is one of the greatest blessings that God in His mercy gives us. It sustained the psalmist when he faced difficulties; if we accept God as our Saviour it will sustain us too.

Thursday, 16 July 2020

As the High Street comes back to life, one of the last set of shops to open again are the charity shops. This is no doubt partly due to lack of volunteers, but slowly most of them are reopening for at least some of the week. They all have their own rules about accepting donations – what they will take, how much and when – and, as I have quite a lot to give them, I spend the afternoon asking them all for the details. It is confusing!

In the evening Vicky and I go for a drink at the local pub. It has a fine beer garden and we sit outside in the sun and enjoy our first refreshment out for exactly four months – the last time was dinner out on 16 March.

Psalm 121:
God will protect us wherever we are

Good morning. We come to one of the best-loved psalms today; it has often inspired musical works, and it provides much comfort to travellers. It was said to be David Livingstone's favourite psalm, and we know from his diaries that he prayed it often on his travels in the heart of Africa. In the set of 15 psalms that forms the Songs of Ascents, we can think of it as being sung by pilgrims as they are on the road to Jerusalem, still far off from the city and with many hills to climb and cross, but already safe under God's protection.

The psalm opens (verse 1) with the traveller asking who will help him on his perilous journey through the hills, and answering himself (verse 2) "My help comes from the Lord, the maker of heaven and earth". And then, for the rest of the psalm, this is elaborated on in a second voice, perhaps a companion who reassures him, or perhaps the traveller himself speaking to his soul to give himself renewed confidence. The Lord is described as watching over the traveller, protecting him and preserving him in a set of three couplets, and the psalm ends (verse 8b) with the wonderful words of comfort "The Lord will watch over your coming and your going, both now and for evermore".

For the psalmist, the great realisation was that God's protection was not limited just to people in Jerusalem, or even those in the land of Israel, but offered to all believers wherever they were – an unusual thought at a time when most people thought of gods as territorial. But the Lord is sovereign over all the earth, for all time – wherever we are, whatever dangers we face, we are safe in His hands.

Friday, 17 July 2020

I add radishes to our growing vegetable garden, sowing some seeds in a space between the beans and courgettes, both of which are by now growing vigorously. As are our cucumbers, and we harvest the first of them for lunch. Apart from some early rhubarb, it is the first of this season's produce we have enjoyed.

Our plumber returns and fashions a panel to cover an access hole through the wall for the shower pipes. It is something we have been meaning to have done for years and, although he is not a professional carpenter, the result is certainly neater than the unsightly hole in the wall we had before. And after I have varnished it, it even looks quite smart.

Psalm 122: A prayer for the city of Jerusalem

Good morning. Today's psalm is a psalm of David, and has as its focus the city of Jerusalem – the city David founded and the destination of the pilgrims whose journey from far off we have studied over the last two days. While yesterday's psalm considered the pilgrim's journey, the hardships he would face on the way and God's presence with him on the road to protect him, today's psalm records his relief and joy at arriving safely at the city, and his wonder at its magnificence compared to the countryside and small villages that typified the rest of Israel.

There is no conflict between the God who is everywhere, as in yesterday's psalm, and the uniqueness of Jerusalem. When David founded the city, he specifically made it a city that belonged to none of the tribes of Israel and so to all of them; a city to bring them together and form the centre of his kingdom. Later, he brought the Ark to his new capital and made it also the centre of the people's faith. David understood well that although God is everywhere, there is something special and uplifting in communal worship, in being together in the presence of God, and it is this that he celebrates in this psalm, as he weaves a picture of a city of homecoming, justice, sanctuary, worship and peace.

For me, it is the start of the psalm that I reflect on most, particularly when we are still unable to "go to the house of the Lord" together. Will I rejoice when the churches are open again? Yes, of course. But once the initial excitement of being back together has passed, will I still be glad at the thought of going to church? How do we view church-going?

As a duty and obligation as Christians, as an opportunity to be with God, as something to look forward to? Or, like the pilgrim and like King David, as all three?

Saturday, 18 July 2020

A day of jam making, as we take advantage of the abundance of raspberries in the shops and make a dozen jars of raspberry jam. Vicky's recipe is remarkably quick and always reliable, and produces a jam with a lovely vibrant red colour.

The international news continues to be dominated by the rapidly rising levels of new cases of the virus – the total tally is now over 14 million worldwide, including over 3 million in the USA. The number of countries re imposing some sort of lockdown is increasing, and it is slightly concerning that here in the UK we appear once again to be out of step as the government prioritises getting the economy back on its feet.

Psalm 123:
Total dependence on God

Good morning. As we continue our study of the Songs of Ascents, the pilgrim's journey continues to bring him closer to God. From his far-off starting point (Psalm 120), he has travelled through the difficult hill country of Judea (Psalm 121), to the holy city of Jerusalem (Psalm 122), and now he is finally able to lift his eyes to the Lord. This was the pilgrim's goal – not Jerusalem, nor even the Temple, but God Himself.

And his first prayer on his arrival is both an affirmation of total dependence on God and a plea for mercy, in this case for relief from the scorn and contempt of non-believers. The psalmist knows his dependence on God is absolute; the words of verse 2a, "As the eyes of slaves look to the hand of their master", may sound slightly jarring to us (indeed in many translations "slaves" is rendered as "servants", though the original text is clearly "slaves"), but the meaning is clear: the psalmist relies completely on God for provision, instruction and correction, and is awaiting His mercy.

The psalms in the Songs of Ascents series are mostly short, powerful psalms. They do stand complete in themselves, but the sense of sequence is also strong. One feature is that they appear to form triplets, beginning with a psalm of trouble (for example Psalms 120 and 123), then moving to a psalm of trust in the Lord (as we saw in Psalm 121), then concluding the triplet with a psalm of triumph and praise (as for example Psalm 122). We will see this pattern continue over the coming days.

For me, today's concise psalm shows that prayers do not have to be long if they are sincere. And I also note that the psalmist makes no demand here, no "hurry up God and show me Your mercy now"; instead he waits patiently, confident that mercy will in due course be shown him at a time of God's choosing. Do I have this patience and trust in God?

Sunday, 19 July 2020

Although much of society is open again (after a fashion), the churches are still faced with great hurdles – gathering for services and social distancing do not fit easily together, and Zoom services are still the norm. I join one today for the congregation at one of the parishes we are patrons of. It is good to be with them, and a lot easier than driving three hours each way to do so in person!

Psalm 124:
Deliverance from destruction

Good morning. Today's psalm is the second in the Songs of Ascents that is attributed to David. The pilgrims have arrived in Jerusalem, and in this psalm they are being led in communal worship. The psalmist shows the leader, perhaps David himself or more likely one of the priests, instructing the people (verse 1b: "let Israel say") to remember their past deliverances, to affirm God's care for His faithful, and to give praise to the Lord. In the triplet of "trouble, trust and triumph", this is a psalm of trust.

It is easy to understand the sentiment of the psalmist behind the opening of this psalm: "If the Lord had not been on our side ...". The people of Israel believed that the Lord was literally "on their side", and they could point to many instances in their history where He had intervened to help them against human enemies. It is perhaps more troubling for us to imagine a God who "takes sides" like this; throughout history wars have resonated to the cry "God is with us", but far too often both sides in a battle have claimed it and it is often the precursor to the most ungodlike slaughter and repression. How can the Almighty, the supreme God of all people, "take sides"?

I prefer to see this as God "taking our side" in humanity's fight with sin; this is a fight that does not divide people but envelopes all of us. All mankind are embroiled in sin, and none can escape without God's help. And now not only the opening of the psalm, which we might paraphrase as "If the Lord had not been on our side, *sin* would have swallowed us alive", but also its close make more sense, and the simple declaration of verse 8: "Our help is in the name of the Lord, the maker of heaven and earth" is not just a statement by the psalmist to the people of Israel, but a statement by all believers to the rest of the unbelieving world.

Monday, 20 July 2020

A better news day on two fronts, as England win an exciting test match to level the series against the West Indies – some stunning cricket, even if it still looks odd on the highlights to see it taking place in an empty stadium – and news of a breakthrough in the search for a vaccine, with some very positive results from tests being carried out in Oxford. The first cheers the soul, though the second may, long term, be more significant!

In the evening I go out stargazing, to see the comet Neowise, one of the brightest for a generation. The sky is clear but the comet is low in the sky, and it is not easy to find somewhere away from the glare of lights. But by waiting till 11.30 pm I do spot it – from our back garden! The tail is clearly visible in my binoculars.

Psalm 125:
Secure in the protection of the Lord

Good morning. The theme of our psalm today is safety and security. The psalmist encourages the faithful by assuring them that they are safe in the secure protection of the Lord, that He surrounds them as the mountains surround Jerusalem. This is a picture of great solidity, and also one of great permanence – the psalm has two time frames, the present and the future, as summarised at the end of verse 2, "now and for evermore".

The true meaning of eternity is extremely difficult for us to understand. We talk of "the everlasting Lord", and we pray in the Lord's prayer that "thine is the kingdom, the power and the glory, for ever and ever" (or, in the more modern version, "now and for ever"), but in every age the faithful have wanted to bring forward God's ultimate triumph, have wanted God to act now, for them. This psalm encourages patience and constancy of faith; in verse 3 the psalmist assures us that "The sceptre of the wicked will not remain over the land allocated to the righteous", in verse 5 that "those who turn to crooked ways the Lord will banish with the evildoers", and in both verses one can certainly feel the emphasis the psalmist is putting on the words "will not" and "will" respectively.

I summarise this psalm for myself as "relax, the Lord is in control and you are safe, now and for ever". It is easier said than done as we live in a turbulent and worrying world, but the promise is there and for those who remain faithful to God, the psalmist assures us that He will remain our Protector and we will inherit His peace.

Tuesday, 21 July 2020

A busy day of business meetings by Zoom, and it is noticeable how more and more people are dressing more smartly for them, with ties and even jackets not now uncommon. The afternoon meeting takes well over two hours, and one realises how physically tiring it is to be sitting in the same position staring at the same screen for so long. A return to meetings in person will be much welcomed!

A good friend – and really quite successful writer of historical novels – has suggested a novel based in the Commonwealth period of Iceland (roughly the 11th and 12th centuries). He invites me to join in the project and share my knowledge of the time to ensure, we hope, that the historical references are not too inaccurate. I have never thought of myself as a writer of fiction, so this could be very interesting!

Psalm 126: Rejoicing at our restoration

Good morning. The main themes of today's psalm are restoration and rejoicing, though, as befits a psalm that is the first in the next triplet of "trouble, trust, triumph", there is also an acceptance of difficult times, in verses 4 and 5, and a prayer for God's assistance to overcome it.

The background to the psalm seems fairly clearly to be the return from Babylon; this fits both with the great joy at the return to Jerusalem (verses 1-3) and also a realisation that the reconstruction task was daunting and would need the blessing of the Lord (verse 4). The psalm thus contains praise for the return, a petition for God's continued oversight of the rebuilding, and confidence that the city will be restored in due course.

This is how I read it at first, though the description is general enough to cover a number of events in Israel's history. But one can also view the psalm as looking forward to our own restoration to God's eternal kingdom, with verse 1, "When the Lord brought back the captives to Zion, we were like men who dreamed", then being a reference to the Resurrection, and Christ's rescue of the faithful from their captivity in sin.

However we choose to read this psalm, as a literal reference to the return from Exile or as a meditation on our own salvation, I can say with the psalmist (verse 3) "The Lord has done great things for me, and I am filled with joy".

Wednesday, 22 July 2020

Today I was introduced to online bridge; Vicky's regular foursome (she has been playing three times a week throughout the lockdown) were one short and I helped them out. It felt rather odd, with Vicky in one room on her laptop, and me in another on mine, doors shut so we could not communicate outside the bridge session! But it was both enjoyable and surprisingly successful: whether by luck or by some algorithm in the program for a new player, we were given hands without too much complexity or too many traps, and I held my own against better and more experienced players well enough.

In the evening we had a second online whisky tasting, this time for the Phoenix Masters, my past masters association. With 18 people on the call, it was another most enjoyable and successful evening, and from the questions that flowed and the general camaraderie, a good innovation for the Phoenix Masters.

Psalm 127:
Life without God is in vain

Good morning. The author of today's psalm is King Solomon, better known as the author of the Book of Proverbs than of psalms, and indeed our psalm today reads very like many of the proverbs. The theme is the centrality of God to a worthwhile life, and how a life without God at its heart will be in vain.

In the first part of the psalm, the focus is on our home, our community and our work. The psalmist does not say that nothing at all can be achieved by man working alone, and far less does he say that we should stop our work and just leave it all to the Lord. The city whose watchmen said "we don't need to bother because the Lord is watching for us" would not survive long! Rather, the psalmist is distinguishing between those who trust in their own endeavours, and those who trust in the Lord; only the latter will see their works truly endure and prosper.

The second part of the psalm moves on to the family. Jewish culture placed, indeed still places today, great emphasis on the family, and the psalmist's original audience would have naturally understood the linkage between these verses on the family and the opening of the psalm: why build a house, why guard a city, why work hard if not for our families? The psalmist says that children are a gift from God (verse 3), and in Jewish culture this psalm was often used to give thanks after the birth of a child.

This is a simple and beautiful psalm of trust; if I trust in the Lord to bless my work and my home, He will make both prosper.

Thursday, 23 July 2020

More and more of the charity shops are re-opening and we donate a large number of CDs to one of them. It is interesting how technology's life-span gets shorter: records were introduced at the end of the 19th century and held sway for nearly 100 years; CDs came in in 1982 and have already been very largely superseded by online streaming services. I wonder what the next technology will be.

In the evening we have a livery dinner. The Basketmakers hold a three-course dinner by Zoom, with everyone dressed up in black tie, everyone joining different sets of people for each course, and the full range of toasts and even speeches, including one from Sheriff Chris Hayward. It is hugely ambitious, hugely successful and great fun, and all without having to travel up to town – the only downside is the washing up after we have finished!

Psalm 128:
The Lord's blessing on the lives of the God-fearing

Good morning. Our psalm this morning is the partner to yesterday's psalm, and continues and deepens our understanding of God's blessing on the families of the faithful. It is also the third psalm in the current triplet of trouble, trust and triumph, and while "triumph" is perhaps rather a strong word for the picture painted here, there is a definite feeling of a bountiful and blessed outcome from the Lord's oversight of our lives.

The psalm is in two parts. The first part, verses 1-4, starts with the psalmist declaring that "Blessed are all who fear the Lord". This sets the theme for the whole psalm, and once again we understand the word "fear" not to mean "be frightened of, run away from" but "revere, be in awe of". Those who do fear God in this sense will seek to obey His commandments or, as the psalmist puts it, "walk in His ways", and they will find that the Lord blesses their life. They will be abundantly provided for and prosperous, and their family life will flourish – the perfect picture of a happy home, centred on God. As the psalmist concludes (verse 4), "Thus is the man blessed who fears the Lord".

The second part of the psalm, verses 5-6, introduces a slightly different note. It is a prayer that those that fear the Lord may indeed receive this blessing, and is a reminder that the Good Life described in the first part of the psalm is not an automatic right, not something we can earn by obedience. Rather, at all times it remains a gift from God, and even for those that fear Him, God's blessings are granted by His grace. So the psalmist does not take God's blessing on the lives of the faithful for granted, but prays that they may receive it.

I cannot demand that God blesses my life. But by fearing Him and obeying His laws I make it possible for Him to enter my life, and His blessings will surely flow.

Friday, 24 July 2020

The first of two livery days, with a committee meeting today by Zoom. It goes well, as indeed we have all come to expect, but the transition to meetings by video conference is surely one of the larger, more dramatic and more quickly assimilated changes that society has ever collectively undertaken and mastered.

In the afternoon I do some more gardening, watering and planting more radishes. As opposed to Zoom meetings, that is something that has not changed much in the last five months – or possibly 500 years!

Psalm 129: Withstanding persecution with the help of the Lord

Good morning. We are back at the start of a new triplet in the Songs of Ascents series this morning, and today's psalm is therefore once again one of trouble. The psalmist speaks of difficult times, but celebrates the fact that the Lord has not forgotten him or allowed his tormentors to triumph over him.

The psalm is in two parts. In the first four verses, the psalmist describes how he has been greatly oppressed, and links his personal suffering to the fate of the nation (verse 1b, "let Israel say"). Verse 3, "Ploughmen have ploughed my back, and made their furrows long", paints a picture of great pain; it is surely prophetic of the scars and furrows on Jesus's back when he was scourged just before His crucifixion. But despite the oppression, the psalmist is not defeated, and he rejoices that the Lord is righteous, and has set him free.

The second part, verses 5-8, is an imprecatory prayer, one of the strongest in the Book of Psalms. The psalmist prays that his oppressors be shamed (verse 5), be few and die early (verses 6-7), and, the most severe of the curses – possibly the harshest curse the psalmist could think of – be without God's blessing (verse 8).

This psalm reminds me that the psalms are not all sweetness and light, praise and rejoicing. There is anger, pain and defiance in this psalm, all proper and wholly justifiable human emotions when directed at those who are wicked. God understands these feelings too; He is with us in our pain, and shares our anger at evil. He will not leave us to succumb to our oppressors.

Saturday, 25 July 2020

Today is St James's Day, the traditional day of the Weavers' Company's annual gathering for Common Hall and lunch. Usually a day of great conviviality and seeing fellow liverymen and old friends but, like so much this year, the physical meeting is cancelled and we migrate to Zoom. The Zoom meeting works well, and the Company runs another quiz – once again I do not trouble the prizegivers!

The weather turns grey in the afternoon and then extremely wet – it wasn't so necessary to spend three hours watering the garden yesterday after all!

Psalm 130:
Trust in the Lord's forgiveness

Good morning. Today we have one of the Penitentiary psalms, in which the psalmist is petitioning God for mercy. It is also the second psalm in our current triplet (Psalms 129, 130 and 131) and so a psalm of trust; the psalmist prays for deliverance with full trust that God will hear his prayer, and so is content to wait for His answer.

The psalm's opening, "Out of the depths I cry to you, O Lord", uses the metaphor of the psalmist floundering and being overwhelmed by his sins as one might be overwhelmed when lost at sea. It is an image we also saw in Psalm 69: in both psalms the hopelessness of the psalmist's position is complete, there is nothing to hold onto and no recourse except to cry out to God. Here the psalmist holds fast to God's promise of forgiveness, and with his trust in this promise he knows his prayer will be answered and declares that he will wait for the Lord to act. Mind you, he does not seem particularly patient in his waiting – verse 6 suggests that, despite his trust that he will in due course be forgiven, he is nevertheless eager for the Lord to act swiftly!

Having put his own trust in the Lord, the psalmist then turns to his countrymen (verses 7-8) and exhorts them to follow him, twice reassuring Israel of the completeness of God's forgiveness and salvation (Verse 7b: "with the Lord … is *full* redemption", verse 8: "He Himself will redeem Israel from *all* their sins").

The Songs of Ascents describe a process of drawing closer to God, both physically (the pilgrimage to Jerusalem) and spiritually, and I am struck by the fact that Psalm 130 comes here, towards the end of the series. It is as if the closer the pilgrim comes to God, the more he realises his sin and his need for God's mercy and forgiveness. Do I know God well enough to realise how much I need Him?

Sunday, 26 July 2020

A grand family picnic today, with everyone congregating at Coombe Hill in the Chilterns to celebrate our daughter Emma's birthday. Much preparation, as we are providing most of the food, tables, chairs, etc, and then a fraught journey, with traffic stationary on the A3, huge tailbacks, heavy rain as we neared our destination, and finally nowhere to park. Lockdown (and the dry spring that accompanied it) is well and truly over! But the picnic was first class (far too much food of course – there always is at our picnics), the rain held off, and the views from Coombe Hill were excellent – one does not think of the Chilterns as having such a dramatic escarpment. A very good day and very nice to see all the family.

Psalm 131: Humility before the Lord

Good morning. Our psalm today is very short, one of three psalms of only three verses, but it has a clear message. It is a psalm of humility, peace of mind and hope; the psalmist is humble before the Lord, and through that has found inner peace and contentment, and finally prays that Israel may find the same peace as he has.

The psalmist is David and, on the surface, it is strange to read Israel's greatest and most successful king declare "I do not concern myself with great matters" (verse 1b). But it is clear that he is lifting his thoughts above his personal life, and even beyond the life of his kingdom. Verse 1 concludes "or things too wonderful for me", suggesting that David is thinking here of the great universal truths, of God's purpose, and simply expressing a trust in the Lord and a willingness to be guided by Him in matters beyond his understanding.

And in doing so, David declares that he has found inner calm, tranquillity, peace. A prize that, for someone whose life was seldom short of adventure and often even in turmoil, was no doubt the one thing he craved most, and, he realised, the one thing that, even when he was king and absolute ruler of Jerusalem, only God could provide.

In our study of the psalms that form the Songs of Ascents we have been observing how they form triplets. Today's psalm is the third in the current triplet and is therefore a psalm of triumph. Compared to some of the other triumphal psalms, it may seem a little low key; but inner contentment is no less of a triumph, no less to be celebrated, no less a blessing from God.

Psalm 46 (verse 10) says "Be still, and know that I am God"; David does this, and is humble before the Lord. And is content.

Monday, 27 July 2020

A visit to the barber today, for the first time since February. New Malden is for some reason blessed with an abundance of barbers, and even with the pent-up demand for their services after so many weeks without, there is almost no wait. Vicky had done an excellent job keeping my hair from getting totally out of control, but it is very nice to have it short, thinned and tidied up again!

Psalm 132: Promises made, promises kept

Good morning. Although we are still in the Songs of Ascents, today's psalm has a slightly different feel: it is longer than the others in the series, the first part of it is more concerned with historical events and, despite the mention of David's many hardships in verse 1, it does not fully fit the triplet pattern of the other psalms we have been studying.

The psalm is a psalm of promises, starting with David's promise to God to create a suitable dwelling-place for Him (verses 2-5), then moving on to God's promise to David that his descendants would rule Israel for ever (verses 11 and 12), and lastly God's promise to His people to dwell with us and give us His salvation (verses 13-18). The psalmist weaves prayer into the psalm as well, between the remembrance of the promises: prayer to remember David (verse 1), prayer for God to come to be with His people in the place prepared for him (verses 6-9) and prayer for the current king (verse 10).

A busy psalm, then! But the unifying theme is "promises made, promises kept". A small part of God's promise to David is conditional – verse 12 declares that *if* David's sons keep the Lord's covenant and statutes they will reign for ever, and we know of course that they didn't and they didn't – but all the rest of God's promises are totally unconditional, including the promise (verse 11b) that "One of your own descendants I will place on your throne", which looks ahead to Jesus as Messiah.

How should I respond to this psalm, to the God who has promised me so much? How can I be among the saints in Zion that (verse 16b) "shall ever sing for joy"?

Tuesday, 28 July 2020

Another sign of how the lockdown and social distancing is changing our lives today, and sometimes for the better. I have a nasty lesion on my back that concerns me, and I ring the doctor to ask for advice. Before the lockdown, one would either have to book an appointment, usually many days in advance, or queue up outside the surgery for an "on-the-day" consultation – these are much in demand and the queue starts forming at 7.45 am, 45 minutes before the surgery opens! But now, they ask me to send photos by email, and promise a call back the next day. Which duly comes, and takes just two to three minutes as the doctor reassures me that it is nothing to worry about. Much better; much more efficient for both me and the doctor.

Like working from home, remote consultations are not perfect – the doctor cannot see what I do not show him, and perhaps something else might have caught his eye that needs attention. But they do work.

Psalm 133:
The blessings of unity

Good morning. Today's psalm is the fourth and last of the psalms in the Songs of Ascents series that is attributed to King David. It is not known for sure when he wrote it, but it might have been when he finally ascended the throne of Israel, after much personal struggle and infighting between the various tribes, and appealed to his people to live in harmony with each other under him.

It would be hard to find anyone who would disagree with the psalm's opening statement. Whether in a family, a community or a church, life is far better when there is unity and harmony rather than discord and strife. The psalmist highlights that unity is both good and pleasant; the original Hebrew words have the meanings of "beneficial" and "enjoyable", and the two are not the same. We can all think of things that are beneficial but not enjoyable, such as discipline, and things that are enjoyable but not beneficial, such as too many jam doughnuts!

The rest of the psalm likens unity to the oil used to anoint the priests, or the dew falling on Mount Hermon (Israel's highest mountain and known for its cool nights, dew and snows in winter, which keep the land around it green all year). These are images of unity as a gift from above, a precious gift, and moreover a gift given in great abundance. And they lead to the last image, which is of the Lord's blessings, poured out on His people for evermore. Just as the priests are drenched in oil and Mount Hermon is drenched in dew, so we are drenched by God's blessings, and His greatest desire for us as brothers and sisters in Christ is that the Church should live in unity.

Unity – a gift from God that we know is good and leads to better lives. But not even the Church, let alone our fallen world, can achieve it. How can I respond to God's gift and help bring about the unity He desires for us?

Wednesday, 29 July 2020

The virus appears to be making a strong return in continental Europe with flare-ups in several places, most notably Spain. The government reintroduces at very short notice a ban on travel to Spain and quarantine for those returning from there, much to the dismay of the travel industry and the inconvenience of those who were on holiday and are now caught, though in truth the government probably had little choice. There is much talk of "a second wave", and how this time it appears to be more younger people being affected – perhaps because they have been quickest to try to resume their normal lives as the lockdown is eased.

Psalm 134:
God's blessing for those who praise Him

Good morning. Today's psalm is the last in our study of the Songs of Ascents, and is a psalm of praise and blessing. It appears to be a call and response, and we can picture the people at the end of the pilgrimage calling out to the priests who remain in the Temple to praise the Lord (verses 1-2), and the priests responding with a blessing (verse 3) for the faithful as they depart. "May the Lord … bless you from Zion", the priests say, and as the pilgrims returned home they will have carried this blessing and the memories of their stay in Jerusalem home with them.

Although like almost all the Songs of Ascents psalms, the psalm is short, it is complete and a suitable ending to the series. It portrays a life of harmony with God; the faithful praise God, and He blesses their lives. This is the culmination of the pilgrimage, and indeed of the Songs of Ascents – it is God's blessing for us that makes possible our pilgrimage to be closer to God, our praise for God, our lives as God's people.

The Songs of Ascents form a wonderful series of psalms; like all the psalms in the Book of Psalms, they are self-contained and complete and can therefore be taken separately, but studied as a sequence they have extra meaning for us on our path through life and in our search for God. For me, they reiterate the fundamental truth that, as a Christian, I am called to live my whole life in the service of the Lord, as an act of worship and so that my life may bring honour and praise to God. Today's psalm reassures us that when we do, God, the Maker of heaven and earth, will bless us and our lives.

Thursday, 30 July 2020

A day of adventure as we join Sam in Putney for coffee by the river and then lunch at a restaurant by the Lower Richmond Road. Our first ventures in actually eating a meal out since the easing of restrictions, and in both cases we sit outside in the sun as possibly less risky, but there the similarity ended! The coffee is delightful; it is excellent coffee, at a café by the new riverside plaza that certainly wasn't there when we lived in Putney 30 years ago and has added greatly to the town. The lunch was alas poor – cleanliness debateable, service slow and erratic (I was initially brought the wrong dish completely) and food really very questionable: my "Greek" salad was centred around a bagel with avocado spread on it and a slice of brie on top! It is difficult to know, unfortunately, how much this is teething troubles as the restaurant tries to get itself back together after the lockdown and how much of it is simply more general incompetence, but Sam is disappointed and not minded to go back to them – there are lots of other places in Putney to try!

Psalm 135:
A hymn of great praise

Good morning. We emerge from the Songs of Ascents, where we have been for the last 15 psalms, to encounter a hymn of great praise to the Lord. Indeed today's psalm and the next one are sometimes seen as a doxology to the Songs of Ascents, with all 17 together given the name "the Great Hallel", or "great praise" (compare to the "Egyptian Hallel" we met in Psalms 113-118). I can picture the pilgrims singing this psalm as they leave Jerusalem and journey home, full of excitement at their time in the city and praise for the God they have just encountered there.

The psalm follows the usual structure of a Praise psalm, with all three key elements present: a call to praise (verses 1-3), reasons for praise (verses 4-18) and a closing instruction to Israel to continue in praise (verses 19-21). The psalmist is keen to give multiple reasons for praising God: His character ("the Lord is good", verse 3), His choice of Israel as His chosen people (verse 4), His supreme sovereignty as the Creator-God (verses 5-7), His rescue of Israel from slavery in Egypt (verses 8-12). He then compares the living Lord to the various worthless and inanimate idols of other nations (verses 15-18, these verses are an echo of Psalm 115 verses 4-8).

For me, this psalm is like a symphonic work – different themes, but all knitted together by the psalmist into one coherent piece, and rising to a crescendo of a conclusion in which the whole psalm reveals its unity and delivers its overall message: "Praise the Lord". And, just as great music will leave you humming the tune to yourself long after the piece has ended, this psalm demands that I allow it to resonate around my head long after I have stopped reading it and closed my Bible for the day. Praise the Lord, indeed!

Friday, 31 July 2020

The hottest day of the year, and my car thermometer shows 44°C, the highest reading I've ever seen. I take more things to the charity shops – with all of Vicky's mother's possessions I have lots to take, but it is a slow process, as they will only accept one or two small boxes at a time (they have limited storage space, and have to leave everything for 72 hours after it has been dropped off to make sure any virus on things has died).

In the afternoon Vicky takes Skittle, the oldest of our three cats and much loved, to the vet. She is completely off her food, and worryingly thin. Alas the vet suspects a cancer; we feared it might be and she may not survive much longer. Still, we have some medicine to make her happier – and it restores her appetite a bit too.

Psalm 136:
Giving thanks for God's unending love

Good morning. Psalm 136 is the partner to Psalm 135, and together they close the "Great Hallel" series of psalms. Whereas Psalm 135 exhorted the faithful to praise the Lord, today's instructs them to give Him thanks. It has a unique construction, as each verse ends with a repeated refrain – it is the only psalm to be written like this, and it was almost certainly to be sung in public worship, with a leader singing the verses and the people responding to each verse with the constant refrain.

The psalm opens with a general call to give thanks (verses 1-3), with verse 1, "Give thanks to the Lord, for He is good. His love endures for ever", a repeat of the last verse of Psalm 118, which closed the last series of Hallel psalms. The psalmist then lists a number of specific reasons to give thanks: God the Creator, God the Deliverer, God the Provider. By this listing and repetition of God's many acts for Israel, the psalm acts like a catechism for the faithful as it goes back and forth from the leader to the people, reminding them of all God's mercy that He has shown them.

The refrain is variously translated in the different versions of the Bible; the NIV, which we have been using in these studies, uses the form "His love endures for ever", but the Hebrew word at the heart of the refrain, *Hesed*, is very much a strong word and is often translated in other versions as mercy or loving kindness. Whichever word is used, after studying this psalm I am left in no doubt of God's devotion to and great care of His people, and in no doubt also that the only possible response is indeed for me to give thanks.

Saturday, 1 August 2020

After Thursday's sally forth into the world of eating out again, we are even more adventurous and go to Langford, a village in West Oxfordshire on the borders of the Cotswolds, for dinner with our daughter Jennifer and her partner James at the local pub, the Bell Inn, and spend the night there. It is charming, and the weather co operates with glorious sun, warm enough not just for drinks out in the evening but breakfast outside the next morning too. There are almost no signs that one can see of the remaining restrictions – no masks, no obvious social distancing. The menus are all accessed by scanning a QR code and reading them online, so we don't have to touch a physical menu but, apart from that, and the ubiquitous hand sanitiser, it is very nice to be about as normal as one can again. And the food was excellent!

The football world has achieved a first today: the English 2019-20 football season is still going (it is the FA Cup Final today), while in Scotland the 2020-21 season has just started with the first round of league games!

Psalm 137:
The lament of the exiles in Babylon

Good morning. Our psalm today is one of the more powerful Imprecatory psalms. It would seem to have been written during the Exile in Babylon, and contains a lament for what the captives have lost (verses 1-4), a vow to remember Jerusalem (verses 5-6), and prayers for judgment (verses 7-9), both on the Edomites (Israel's neighbours, who, instead of assisting them in their struggle with the Babylonians, joined in the attack and exulted at Jerusalem's fall) and more seriously on the Babylonians themselves, for whom the psalmist declares their doom and praises those who will mete out punishment on them.

The opening words of the psalm are well known, having been used by several people in a song of the same name, most famously the group Boney M, whose cover version of the Jamaican original sold over two million copies in 1978 in the UK alone. But the modern song has an interesting omission: it only refers to the first six verses of the psalm, the lament and the vow to remember, and it pointedly excludes the imprecatory prayer.

What then, as Christians, are we to make of verses 7-9? There is no sign here of forgiving one's enemies, of turning the other cheek; instead the verses resonate with anger, hatred and a desire for revenge. And even though Boney M omitted them, the Bible does not; they are there in full and for a purpose. The answer must be that it is in the Bible to encourage us to be honest when we pray to God: if we are angry, we should tell Him we are angry, as there is no point in a psalm full of harmony and praise when inside we are burning with hatred and rage. Since He sees what is in our heart anyway, it would be a pointless pretence!

This psalm teaches me that I should share my whole life with God, all of my emotions. Only then will God be able to help me whatever my feelings, only then can He enable me to overcome them and return closer to Him.

Sunday, 2 August 2020

A comfortable night at the Bell Inn and a lazy breakfast outside in the sun to round off a most enjoyable short stay in the Cotswolds. And an easy journey home in light traffic.

The hot weather is proving too much for our ancient fridge and, for the second time in a few days, the milk has curdled. So we bite the bullet and order a new one. Delivery is set for a week and a half – fingers crossed!

Psalm 138: Praising God for His steadfast care

Good morning. For the final time in our study of the Book of Psalms we meet a set of psalms attributed to King David. He is recorded as the author of most of the psalms in Books I and II of the Psalter, and so these eight psalms towards the end of Book V, Psalms 138-145, help to bind the whole collection together.

There is no indication of any specific occasion for the psalm; instead David is looking both back and forward – back with thankfulness to what God has done for him (verse 3: "When I called You answered me"), and forward with confidence to God's continuing care and protection (verse 8: "The Lord will fulfil His purpose for me; Your love, O Lord, endures for ever"). And both move him to declare his praise.

Woven in with this praise for what God has done, David includes praise for what God is, for His love and faithfulness (verse 2a) and for His name and His Word (verse 2b). At a time when most other peoples praised their gods for their strength, their power and their might, David chooses to praise the Lord for His very different qualities of mercy and faithfulness, and holding to His word and covenant. David knew well how precious this was; as an absolute ruler himself he knew he could at any time change his mind and his subjects would just have to accept it, so he valued God's constancy and steadfastness and praised Him for it.

For me, all of David's qualities shine through this psalm: his humility before the Lord and realisation of his total reliance on Him, his gratitude for God's love and mercy, his desire to respond with thanksgiving, his boldness in praising the Lord in public (verse 1: "I will praise You, O Lord, with all my heart; before the gods I will sing Your praise"), and finally his desire that all the earth might join Israel in praising God (verses 4 and 5). An inspiring picture of a life lived for the Lord.

Monday, 3 August 2020

A busy day online as I first have a long session with the illustrator of a book I am writing on Market Axioms – he is making excellent progress and it is exciting to see the project coming to life – then the resumption of one of the bible study groups I belong to at our church, then three hours of online bridge in the afternoon, filling in again for one of Vicky's usual foursome who is absent. Not quite as successful as last time, but we scramble to a draw by the close. And with relief I turn the computer off for the evening!

Today the domestic football season finally ends, with the final game. It has never run into August before!

Psalm 139:
Total surrender to the omniscient God

Good morning. Today we have another psalm of David; it is an intensely personal psalm, and possibly the most complete description of David's theology, his understanding of God, as it explores both the greatness of God's character and His involvement in and direction of David's life.

The main part of the psalm consists of David's meditation on three aspects of God: God the all-knowing (verses 1-6), God the always-present (verses 7-12), God the all-powerful (verses 13-16). In effect, David is saying to God "You know me, You see me and are with me, You created me and control my life" – indeed in verses 15 and 16 David looks both at the time before he was born and far into the future, and realises that God had planned out everything, his entire life.

And how does David respond to this omniscient, omnipresent and omnipotent God? In George Orwell's book *Nineteen Eighty-Four* there is a similar all-pervasive power in Big Brother, and in the novel the natural reactions to him are fear and a desire to hide. But David's response to God is the complete opposite: God's thoughts are precious to him (verses 17-18), God's enemies dismay and disgust him (verses 19-22) and he implores the all-seeing God to search him ever more closely, to purify him of any remaining sins (verses 23-24). Even the small section of imprecation against the wicked (verse 19: "If only You would slay the wicked, O God"), which otherwise might be thought slightly jarring in a psalm centred on God's greatness, is driven by David's zeal for the Lord.

But alongside David's great understanding of God's nature, this is above all a psalm of great trust, of total surrender to God's control over every aspect of his life. It challenges us – it challenges me – to live our life similarly under God's direction and protection. What would my life look like if I were to do this as completely as David?

Tuesday, 4 August 2020

Another re-entry into normal life as I go out to lunch with a friend at a local restaurant. It is three miles away, and I choose to walk – I have yet to venture onto public transport again and it is a pleasant walk both ways. The restaurant is relatively busy, but again one notices how very different the different arrangements each place decides to adopt are – no face masks for the waiting staff for example. The meal is covered by the government's subsidy scheme, and so for a full roast carvery, a drink and coffee I pay just £6.00!

Psalm 140:
A plea to be rescued from evil men of violence

Good morning. We continue in our final set of psalms written by David, and today's psalm is a flashback to many of his other psalms earlier in the Psalter. David is once again facing difficulties, and the psalm follows the pattern we have seen before of complaint to the Lord setting out his problems, prayer to the Lord for help, trust that the Lord will protect him and a final call to praise.

There is an urgency to this psalm; there is no prelude of praise or meditation on the Lord, and instead David gets to the point straight away with his opening words "Rescue me, O Lord". And as well as wanting to be rescued, David asks the Lord to keep him safe (verse 4, "Keep me, O Lord, from the hands of the wicked") – he knows that God will deliver him from the evil men, the men of violence attacking him, but he also knows that they will not magically melt away and that he will therefore continue to need the Lord's protection.

This does not however stop him praying that the wicked will both fail (verse 8) and be cast down (verses 9-11). I note that the prayer for the wicked to not succeed is based on the fact that if they do succeed, they will become proud; we can imagine them saying "Who needs God, we are greater than God", and thereby both diminishing reverence for the Lord among the people and turning the people away from Him.

As so often in these Petitionary psalms, David concludes by keeping his focus fully on the Lord, and declaring that He is worthy of praise. There is a great sense of the centrality of God to David's life here: at this point in his life David has yet to enjoy much success or authority, and indeed most of the time he is facing hardship and danger – but his trust in the Lord remains complete.

Wednesday, 5 August 2020

A quiet day as I take more boxes to the charity shops – it is a drawn-out process as they only have room to take one or two small boxes a day, but I have not many to go now – catch up on video talks I have set aside to watch (there are so many good talks online now that I struggle to find time for all of them!) and then go round our vegetables, which are all nicely coming due for harvesting. We have some of our courgettes with dinner tonight, and very nice too.

One of the City catering companies announces a return to dining in livery halls. I ask for details, but alas the social distancing at the table is so large that it rather negates the point of getting together!

Psalm 141:
The battle against temptation and sin

Good morning. We have another Petitionary psalm of David this morning, as he once again seeks God's help, but whereas yesterday's psalm was concerned with David's enemies and the dangers they posed for him, today's is concerned with the enemy within: temptation. And whereas yesterday's psalm was one of extreme urgency, starting with the cry "Rescue me, O Lord", today's starts with a more considered – though no less heartfelt – appeal to God to hear his prayer.

For me, this shows David's understanding of the nature of the battle against sin and temptation; while the battle against human enemies may be sharp and require urgent help, it is often short, but the battle against sin is a long, continuous campaign. David knows that this is the real battle he faces, not against others who wish to harm his physical life, but against his own sinful nature which threatens to harm his spiritual life. It is, literally, a matter of life and death for him. So he pleads with God for his prayer to be heard and accepted (verses 1-2), describes at length the help he needs (verses 3-4) and says he will willingly accept rebuke and discipline (verse 5: "Let a righteous man strike me", or even more direct in some translations: "Let the Righteous One strike me") if he falls short in the struggle.

The psalm includes a brief prayer against the wicked (verses 6-7) but in the concluding verses David returns to the main theme of the psalm, keeping his eyes on God, his only defence against sinning, and praying that he may be spared from temptation – verse 9, "Keep me from the snares they have laid for me, from the traps set by the evildoers".

This psalm reminds me forcefully of the real battle I face, the ongoing struggle against sin and my sinful nature. 1,000 years before Christ gave us the Lord's Prayer, with its line "Lead us not into temptation", David has identified his and our real enemy – the enemy within.

Thursday, 6 August 2020

A disappointment as the radishes I planted three weeks ago, while growing good leafage, appear not to be growing any actual radishes! Alas, and not sure why. In the afternoon we go to a friend who lives nearby and enjoy a very pleasant drink in their garden; it is a very hot afternoon, but nice to sit outside in the shade (and more reassuring in these strange times than meeting other people indoors).

Psalm 142:
God our only refuge when crisis overwhelms

Good morning. Today's psalm is headed "Of David, when he was in the cave", and refers to the time when David was hiding from Saul and took refuge in a cave. It is thus the partner to Psalm 57, composed in the same adverse circumstances. But whereas in the earlier psalm David was praying confidently to the Lord, with a steadfast heart and assured of His protection, this psalm is altogether a more desperate prayer.

Running throughout the psalm is a sense of David's helplessness and hopelessness; he is depressed, deserted by his friends and close to admitting defeat. He turns to God as his only hope of help; the contrast between verse 4, "Look to my right and see; no one is concerned for me. I have no refuge; no one cares for my life", and verse 5, "I cry to You, O Lord; I say, 'You are my refuge'", is complete.

This is an intense prayer, entirely in the first person and clearly from someone at the end of their resistance. It moves from the semi-calm tone of verse 1, where David merely says that "I cry aloud to the Lord; I lift up my voice to the Lord for mercy", to the more direct verse 5, "I cry to You, O Lord", to the urgent demands of verses 6 and 7, "Listen to my cry", "Rescue me", "Set me free". We can hear the emotion in his voice, the rising desperation.

So many people turn to God in prayer only as a last resort; they only look up when they are flat on their back. What distinguishes David is that he maintained a full dialogue with God through good times and bad; this gave him the knowledge of how to pray to God, the assurance that God would listen and the confidence that God would act. How is my prayer life – in a box marked "For use in emergencies" or one labelled "Use several times daily"?

Friday, 7 August 2020

Another extremely hot day, with the thermometer reaching 36°C in SW London (and 45°C in the car when I go out to the shops!). Not quite as hot as people were fearing, and not quite the hottest day Britain has ever seen – that remains 38.7°C, seen in Cambridge in July last year – but still very stifling and enervating. A day for doing not very much … slowly!

Psalm 143:
Teach me to know You better, to do Your will

Good morning. Once again we have a psalm of David this morning, and once again he is in difficulty, surrounded by enemies, though unlike yesterday's psalm there is no indication of which specific occasion in David's life prompted the prayer.

This psalm is unusual as one of the Petitionary psalms in that it spends comparatively little time describing David's enemies or his current predicament, and focuses much more on David's own feelings and his relationship with God. Thus although David's enemies are mentioned in verse 3 ("The enemy pursues me, he crushes me to the ground; he makes me dwell in the darkness like those long dead"), verse 9 ("Rescue me from my enemies, Lord, for I hide myself in You") and verse 12 ("In Your unfailing love, silence my enemies; destroy all my foes, for I am Your servant"), these are limited and somewhat generic references; indeed it is not even clear that they are human enemies at all, and the psalm could also be read as a prayer for help against Satan and rescue from sin.

But whatever his enemies, there is no doubt in David's mind that he needs help. He begs not to be judged (verse 2), as he knows he is sinful; he expresses his extreme need for the Lord (verse 6, "my soul thirst for You like a parched land"); he implores God to answer him quickly (verse 7); he asks for instruction and guidance in the Lord's ways and how to do His will (verses 8 and 10).

What a lesson on how to pray this is for us. For many people, prayer can, if they are not careful, degenerate into a sort of shopping list – "O Lord, please do this, and please do that". But David's response to his difficulties and challenges is to offer a much more humble and obedient prayer that not only asks for relief from the current danger, but also and more importantly seeks to know God better.

Saturday, 8 August 2020

Today we visit my cousins in Hampshire for an al-fresco lunch; the day is hot and still, and we spend a lovely lazy afternoon in their garden sitting in the shade of their arbour. Such a simple pleasure, but made all the better for being able to do so again after months when we couldn't.

Another test series starts, this time against Pakistan and, after the excitements of the well-contested three-match series against the West Indies, we have another nail-biting finish and unexpected England victory. Despite the absence of a crowd at the ground, it is great cricket; the current England side is full of exciting players.

Psalm 144:
Praise for the God of both war and peace

Good morning. In contrast to the last few days' psalms, which have seen David urgently calling upon God in times of difficulty, danger and despair, we have a calmer prayer here. It seems to have been written early in his time as king: it is a "new song" (verse 9), sung "to the One who gives victory to kings, who delivers His servant David from the deadly sword" (verse 10).

The psalm is a mixture of petition, meditation and praise. Dangers still remain; David knows that he still needs the Lord as his rock and stronghold (verses 1-2), and calls on Him to be his leader in battle (verses 5-8). And he still has specific enemies that he, and Israel, need help to overcome (verse 11). But he also has time to reflect and marvel on the fact that God cares about man: verses 3-4 ask "O Lord, what is man that You care for him, the son of man that You think of him? Man is like a breath; his days are like a fleeting shadow".

This is an echo of Psalm 8, another psalm of David where he asked the same question but in a slightly different context. In Psalm 8, the emphasis was on God the all-powerful Creator, and the wonder that someone so omnipotent is concerned with man; here, the emphasis is instead on God the mighty Warrior, but David's amazement that God should care about humanity, should care about him personally, is the same.

David is so confident that the Lord will give Israel victory that he concludes the psalm (verses 12-15) with praise for the coming prosperity of his kingdom. There is no doubt in these verses; they paint a picture of peace and plenty, and well may David conclude "Blessed are the people of whom this is true". But it is also a wonderful promise for us: "There will be … no going into captivity, no cry of distress … blessed are the people whose God is the Lord".

Sunday, 9 August 2020

Even in the hottest weather we like to maintain the tradition of a Sunday roast lunch, but in a concession to another very hot day, we move the garden table under the shade of the tree and eat it outdoors. It is very pleasant, and quite cool in the shade and, as an extra bonus, our daughter Jennifer joins us; she has spent the weekend in Putney and drops by on her way home.

Psalm 145: Praising God for who He is and what He does

Good morning. For the last time we encounter a psalm of David and, after all his trials and difficulties, which he has survived with the guidance and protection of the Lord, it is proper that it is a psalm of praise. It marks the start of the final set of "Hallel" psalms, Psalms 145-150, a doxology of praise that closes the Psalter. It is also the only psalm in the entire Book of Psalms to be formally entitled "A psalm of praise".

David gives many different reasons in this psalm why he, and we, should praise God. He starts by praising God for who He is (verse 3: "Great is the Lord"), His splendour and majesty, and His mighty works (verses 4-6), and he celebrates God's goodness and righteousness (verse 7). He then moves to praising God for His mercy and compassion, and His great grace (verses 8-13a). He praises God's faithfulness to His people, and His care of them (verses 13b-16). Finally, David returns to reflecting on God's righteousness again (verses 17-20), before closing with an exhortation that "every creature praise His holy name for ever and ever" (verse 21).

What a wonderful litany of reasons to praise God. This psalm had a special place in Jewish liturgy, as it was the custom to recite it twice in the morning and once in the evening; it was a reminder for the faithful of both the nature of God and of His actions; who He is and what He does. It is also a reminder that God is an *active* God, seeking to be part of our lives and not, like some deities, a far off person separate from us and disinterested in us.

What reasons will I have to praise God and give Him thanks today?

Monday, 10 August 2020

Another very hot day indeed – we try to buy some fans but naturally nowhere has any, they are all out of stock!

In the afternoon Vicky takes part in the annual Inter-Livery bridge competition; this is usually a mixture of serious bridge and social gathering, complete with a nice dinner, but like so much it has migrated online. The online arrangement works and the bridge is good, even if not the same as four around a table, but one does sadly miss the social side of so many of these annual events.

Psalm 146:
Let me praise the Lord all my life

Good morning. The final five psalms in the Book of Psalms both start and end with the phrase "Praise the Lord". Throughout our studies of the psalms to date, we have met the full range of human emotions: praise, wonder and gratitude, but also fear, shame, grief, doubt and anger. We have seen confident faith and struggling faith, we have seen the psalmists facing defeat and destruction and celebrating deliverance and victory. But in these last five psalms there are no longer any doubts or fears, just praise for the Lord.

Today's psalm is the most personal of the five, the only one in which the psalmist refers to himself (verse 1b: "Praise the Lord, O my soul", verse 2a: "I will praise the Lord all my life"). He cautions against trusting in princes, or men of power, and contrasts them with the care of the Lord; verses 5-9 outline the many ways in which God cares for His people, and behind every verse is the unspoken comment "and princes don't do this for you".

As we will see over the coming days, the five psalms together describe ever widening circles of praise, moving from today's personal statement to Psalm 147, which calls on Jerusalem to praise the Lord, to Psalm 148, which describes praise from heaven and earth, to Psalm 149, in which Israel and the assembly of the saints is called to praise, to the final psalm, Psalm 150, with its closing command "Let everything that has breath praise the Lord". A magnificent and all-encompassing vision of praise.

But for today we are able to stay at the personal level, and repeat with the psalmist “I will sing praise to my God as long as I live”.

Tuesday, 11 August 2020

The heatwave continues, and the weather has become very humid as well. Most unpleasant, and it is causing people to reassess the merits of working from home. For those stuck in small and crowded flats with neither a garden nor air conditioning, the office, with its space and cool air, suddenly seems rather more attractive after all!

The resumption of sport continues, but also continues to be at risk from the virus. Both football in Scotland and Rugby League in England find that they may have restarted too soon: both have recorded teams with people testing positive for the virus and have had to postpone some matches. Two steps forward for both a couple of weeks ago, but now one step back; getting the balance right will not be easy.

Psalm 147:
Let Jerusalem praise the Lord

Good morning. Today's psalm is another psalm of praise, and after the emphasis on personal praise in yesterday's psalm, here the psalmist calls on the city of Jerusalem to praise the Lord. There is much evidence that the psalm was written soon after the return of the first Jews from the Exile in Babylon, for example verse 1b: "How good is it to sing praises to our God", verses 2-3: "The Lord builds up Jerusalem; He gathers the exiles of Israel. He heals the broken-hearted and binds up their wounds", and verses 12-14: "Extol the Lord, O Jerusalem … He strengthens the bars of your gates … blesses your people within you … grants peace to your borders". All of this would have encouraged the returning Israelites as they set about rebuilding their city.

The psalm contains three separate calls to praise the Lord, in verses 1, 7 and 12, and after each the psalmist gives us many reasons for doing so. Interwoven with the specific references to Jerusalem, and God's care for His city, are references to the Lord as God the Creator (for example verses 4-5 and 15-18), God the Provider (verses 8-9) and God the Lawgiver (verses 19-20).

It is the last of these references that stands out for me. The psalmist declares that God "has revealed His word to Jacob, His laws and decrees to Israel. He has done this for no other nation; they do not know His laws". Law, and the accompanying discipline that it implies, is not necessarily the first thing one would think of to ask for from one's deity, nor at times very enjoyable, but God's faithful had learnt to understand it, appreciate it and on numerous occasions return to it after experiencing the alternative of lawlessness and Godlessness, and verse 20 is said not with pride but with wonder at how Israel had been singled out to receive such a valuable gift.

The psalmist understands the value of God-given laws, and is in no doubt that they are a cause to Praise the Lord.

Wednesday, 12 August 2020

We spend all day waiting for rain: the clouds gather, there is thunder, near neighbours no more than 10 miles away report rain, further afield there is heavy rain and alas renewed floods. But in New Malden it remains stubbornly dry. It is however very slightly cooler by the evening, thank goodness.

Psalm 148: Let heaven and earth praise the Lord

Good morning. The circles of praise continue to widen in today's psalm, from the personal in Psalm 146, to the call to Jerusalem yesterday in Psalm 147, to today's exhortation to the whole of heaven and earth. The psalm is a straightforward command; the psalmist does not dwell overlong on why all of creation should praise the Lord, he just states it as a self-evident universal duty.

I find the simplicity of this psalm very refreshing. Many of the Praise psalms we have studied, in this closing sequence of psalms but also earlier in the Psalter, refer to what God has done, either for the psalmist in person or for His people Israel; they talk of His great compassion and mercy, of His rescue of His people, of His ongoing involvement in their lives. In this psalm, the psalmist encourages us instead to praise God for what He is. It is a simpler approach to a Supreme Deity, and reminds me of the close of Charles Wesley's great hymn "Love divine, all loves excelling", the last verse of which is:

Finish, then, Thy new creation;
Pure and spotless let us be.
Let us see Thy great salvation
Perfectly restored in Thee;
Changed from glory into glory,
Till in Heav'n we take our place,
Till we cast our crowns before Thee,
Lost in wonder, love, and praise.

The psalmist is indeed "lost in wonder, love, and praise" in this psalm, and invites us to be too. What part am I going to play today in this universal praise for the Lord?

Thursday, 13 August 2020

The fridge we ordered on 2 August arrives, and looks very good. The doors need turning round, a task that "is simple to do and should take the average person about 15 minutes". An hour and a half later we prove that it is not simple at all (and/or that we are not average people), but we are finally successful.

In international news, New Zealand has had to reimpose a lockdown in Auckland with four new cases of the virus confirmed. This is after 102 days without a single case of virus transmission. It begs the question – how many people, even in New Zealand, have had it all along but have not shown any symptoms? Asymptomatic transmission is a real danger, as it can't be detected or therefore easily traced or stopped.

Psalm 149:
Let all the saints praise the Lord

Good morning. The penultimate psalm in the Psalter is not just a call to praise but also a call to arms. The psalm opens with the usual declaration "Praise the Lord", and the first few verses expand on this instruction – Israel is not just to praise the Lord, but also to rejoice while doing so. It is described as a joyous act, with music and dancing. The Bible is often clearer on our duty to praise God than it is on instructions how, but here the people of Israel are given clear guidance about how to praise the Lord, and also left in no doubt that the objective is for them to enjoy doing so. And finally, that if they rejoice while praising God, then God will in His turn receive their praise with delight. What a wonderful picture that is.

But then in verse 6 the psalm takes a slightly unexpected turn, as the people with praise filling their mouths are exhorted also to carry a double-edged sword in their hands. They are to be not just a choir hymning the Lord, but His army on earth, opposing evil and forging His kingdom. When we pray in the Lord's Prayer "Thy kingdom come", a prayer that includes not only the glorification of the righteous but also the concomitant destruction of the wicked, it is sometimes easy to understand this as the faithful merely willing it to happen, looking forward to its arrival. But faith is not a spectator sport, and in this psalm, the psalmist is in no doubt of the part that the faithful are expected to play in bringing about God's kingdom.

Running through this psalm is a strong sense of fellowship between God and His faithful people – the psalm uses the word "saints" three times to describe the faithful: privileged to be in assembly with God (verse 1b), rejoicing at their salvation from God (verse 5) and glorified for leading the creation of God's kingdom on earth (verse 9a). Privilege, joy, glory – the reward of faith. Are you among the saints? Am I?

Friday, 14 August 2020

The weather has well and truly broken, and the very hot spell – nearly a week of temperatures in the mid to high 30s, the longest such run in the UK ever – gives way to several bursts of heavy rain. Much relief for the garden! The combination of a hot summer, plus my newly-installed irrigation and watering system (see 19 May), has served our vegetables well: we have a good crop of almost all of them, especially the beetroots, and only the radishes are a little disappointing.

Psalm 150:
Let everything that has breath praise the Lord

Good morning. We come today to the last psalm in the Psalter and, just as each of the first four books of the Book of Psalms ends with a doxology of praise – the last verses of Psalms 41, 72, 89 and 106 – so the whole of Psalm 150 can be seen as a doxology that brings to a close both Book V and the entire Psalter.

In six verses the psalmist mentions the word "praise" no less than 13 times, and in every case it is an instruction. We are instructed *where* to praise God – in His sanctuary, and in His mighty heavens (in other words, everywhere); we are instructed *why* to praise God – for His acts of power and His surpassing greatness (in other words, for what He has done and who He is); we are instructed *how* to praise God – on every kind of musical instrument (in other words, with everything we have and in every way we can); and finally we are instructed *who* should praise God – "Let everything that has breath praise the Lord".

It is a comprehensive list, and the Temple sounds as though it would have been a noisy place! The list of instruments is purposefully wide, because each instrument was traditionally played by a different class of people. Some were reserved for the priests, some for men, some for women (shades of our modern orchestras, where almost without exception harpists are female and trombonists are male!), and the psalmist is re-emphasising with the list that *everyone* has a part to play in praising the Lord.

The Book of Psalms starts with a psalm of six verses that opens with the words "Blessed is the man" and presents us with a choice: the way of the world or the way of God. It ends with another psalm of six verses that offers the only possible conclusion for anyone who chooses the way of God, closing with the words "Praise the Lord". From "Blessed is the man" to "Praise the Lord", the Psalter offers a true guide to our journey through life. It makes me ask myself, have I made it my journey, have I chosen the way of God, will I praise the Lord?

Saturday, 15 August 2020

We hold a family lunch for Sam's birthday today – his actual birthday is in March, and was right at the start of the lockdown, and it is only now that we have been able to all gather together. And we receive news of how our church plans to restart Sunday meetings. Two events we have had to put on hold for five months and, at the end of this journey through the Book of Psalms, two signs of the ongoing return to normality.

The Book of Psalms in our lives

The Book of Psalms is unique. In the rest of the Bible God speaks to us: through His words, through His actions, through His law, through His prophets and, in the New Testament, through His apostles and, most wondrously and directly of all, through His Son Jesus. Alongside being a God who *cares* for His people, and who *commits* to us through His covenant, He is first and foremost a God who wishes to *communicate* with us.

But in the Book of Psalms, we hear the voices of men speaking to God. We hear the other side of the relationship between God and man – for it is a two-way relationship – and we hear in the 150 psalms every human emotion. By reading and studying the psalms we learn that there is nothing that cannot be brought to God, laid before Him, left in His care. There is nothing we are not allowed to say, no point in trying to hide what we are feeling – indeed, He will see and know it anyway.

Many people have found in the Book of Psalms examples of ways we can speak to God, whatever we are facing in life. There are psalms for when we are happy, and psalms for when we are sad. There are psalms for when we are full of wonder and overcome with God's mercy and grace, but also for when we are fearful, or ashamed, or despairing, or angry – even when we are angry with God Himself.

Most good study bibles will suggest a list of psalms to turn to for any situation you may be facing, and the internet is a vast source of advice: typing "a psalm for when I feel ..." into an internet search engine will always produce suggestions and psalms to read. They may be well over 2,000 years old, and in some cases over 3,000 years old, but human emotions have changed very little and they are just as fresh and as relevant, just as helpful and comforting, as they were when they were first written.

And on top of that, they are written in some of the most beautiful poetry in the Bible. Whether you read the psalms for advice and guidance, for comfort and reassurance, or simply to marvel at their beauty, I hope that they will always be something you enjoy turning to, and a guide to bring you closer to the Lord who inspired their authors to write them.

Thematic index to the commentaries

One of the features of the psalms is that despite being songs and prayers on similar themes, each psalm is in its own way unique. I have tried to mark this by giving each day's commentary a different title; these titles are listed below to help you find the precise psalm for whatever occasion you are faced with or feelings you might have.

Psalm 19: God's creation reveals His greatness
Psalm 20: A prayer for victory in battle
Psalm 21: Praise after victory has been won
Psalm 22: From great suffering to great joy
Psalm 23: The Lord is my shepherd
Psalm 24: God the glorious and eternal King
Psalm 25: A prayer for guidance and pardon
Psalm 26: Commitment to God
Psalm 27: Unwavering confidence in God's blessings
Psalm 28: Calling on God for help
Psalm 29: A hymn of praise
Psalm 30: A psalm of celebration
Psalm 31: Trust in the Lord
Psalm 32: The blessing of forgiveness
Psalm 33: Praise to the Creator God
Psalm 34: Reliance on the Lord at all times
Psalm 35: A prayer for help against one's enemies
Psalm 36: A contemplation on God
Psalm 37: The fates of the wicked and the faithful compared
Psalm 38: Sorrow for sin, and a plea for restoration
Psalm 39: The emptiness of life without God
Psalm 40: Waiting patiently for the Lord
Psalm 41: A prayer when feeling sick or abandoned
Psalm 42: Meditating on the need for God
Psalm 43: Putting our hope in God
Psalm 44: A plea for help from the battle-weary
Psalm 45: On the occasion of the king's wedding
Psalm 46: God our refuge and strength
Psalm 47: God is the king of the whole earth
Psalm 48: God's holy city is secure
Psalm 49: The futility of relying on worldly possessions
Psalm 50: The judgment of God, the importance of faith

Psalm 83: A call to God for help against many enemies
Psalm 84: Longing to be with God
Psalm 85: A prayer for renewal and restoration
Psalm 86: A devoted servant calls on his Master
Psalm 87: Zion city of God
Psalm 88: A prayer from the depths of despair
Psalm 89: God's everlasting covenant
Psalm 90: The eternal nature of God
Psalm 91: God's protective care
Psalm 92: The joy of praising the Lord
Psalm 93: The Lord reigns
Psalm 94: God the righteous Judge
Psalm 95: A call to worship, a sermon from God
Psalm 96: Sing praise to God the eternal Ruler
Psalm 97: God's awesome power
Psalm 98: A call to praise the Lord
Psalm 99: God is holy
Psalm 100: A universal summons to praise and thank God
Psalm 101: Blueprint for a righteous reign, a blameless life
Psalm 102: Pouring out one's woes to God
Psalm 103: Praise the Lord O my soul
Psalm 104: Sing praises to God the Creator
Psalm 105: God the Sovereign Actor in Israel's history
Psalm 106: Israel's repeated disobedience
Psalm 107: God's care of His people through the ages
Psalm 108: Confidence in God's victories
Psalm 109: Calling for God's vengeance on the wicked
Psalm 110: God the Father speaks to Christ the Messiah
Psalm 111: Sing praises for God's works
Psalm 112: God's blessings for the righteous
Psalm 113: Praise for the supreme God who cares for His people
Psalm 114: A poetic recalling of the Exodus

Psalm 141: The battle against temptation and sin
Psalm 142: God our only refuge when crisis overwhelms
Psalm 143: Teach me to know You better, to do Your will
Psalm 144: Praise for the God of both war and peace
Psalm 145: Praising God for who He is and what He does
Psalm 146: Let me praise the Lord all my life
Psalm 147: Let Jerusalem praise the Lord
Psalm 148: Let heaven and earth praise the Lord
Psalm 149: Let all the saints praise the Lord
Psalm 150: Let everything that has breath praise the Lord

Lightning Source UK Ltd.
Milton Keynes UK
UKHW010639200421
382299UK00002B/254

9 781916 387362